Cooking for compliments

by Ruth Morgan
cookery editor of Woman

Hamlyn
London · New York · Sydney · Toronto

ILLUSTRATED ON THE JACKET:
Salmon Cream in Lemon Cups, see page 8
Watercress Cream Soup, see page 15
Lamb Guard of Honour, see page 65
Lemon Chicken Pie, see page 73
Coffee Party Mousse, see page 117
Fruit Trifles, see page 119

ACKNOWLEDGEMENTS:
Jacket photograph by Iain Reid
China featured on the jacket is
Mason's Ironstone – Manchu design
(A member of the Wedgwood Group)

Illustrations by Robert Murdoch of "Group Six"
© Copyright Odhams Press Ltd., 1968
Reprinted 1975

ISBN 0 600 03962 5

THE HAMLYN PUBLISHING GROUP LTD.,
London · New York · Sydney · Toronto
Astronaut House, Feltham, Middlesex, England
Printed in England by Jarrold and Sons Ltd., Norwich

Contents

Cooking for compliments

This is a personal cook book. It is Wooden Spoon Club's choice of all our favourite recipes—the ones we enjoy serving to our families and friends. You'll discover many new dishes, all chosen for ease of preparation and superb flavour. And you'll find some of the old favourites, some we just couldn't leave out, polished up and at their best—just as all the recipes have been tried, tested and perfected in the Wooden Spoon Club kitchens.

But this is more than a book of recipes—it is a complete guide to kitchen know-how and successful entertaining. Among each collection of main dishes, you'll find a page with a Golden Border. Here you'll turn up our Chef's Special—a mouthwatering dish to turn your mid-day or evening party into a memorable banquet. So, if you're looking for something to tempt and impress your guests, watch for the Golden Border.

The Turquoise Border indicates another bonus. It shows the Menu pages. Flip over to one, and you'll find a carefully thought-out menu, based around main dishes in this book. Follow a menu, and you can be sure to give guests a carefully balanced meal, each dish complementing the other.

We've remembered something else: that time and time again you've asked us for help in preparing the everyday things. For you know, as we do, that there is a right way to make even the simplest dish—indeed, some of the so-called simple dishes are often tricky. So, right through the book, you'll find our simple sketch strips, a clear and concise guide to the expert touches that make all the difference.

Whatever kind of cook you are—whether a beginner or a fully-fledged hostess—this is the book for you. We designed it with *you* in mind—and it comes to you from Wooden Spoon Club with the best of cook's compliments.

Ruth Morgan

Cookery Editor of **Woman**

1
Starters

Melon and prawn cocktail (*recipe overleaf*)

Starters

Melon and prawn cocktail

SERVES: SIX

1 large honeydew melon
juice of ½ lemon
few unpeeled prawns

PRAWN MAYONNAISE:

½ teaspoon caster sugar
pinch each of salt, freshly ground
  black pepper and dry mustard
1 egg yolk
1 tablespoon lemon juice
¼ pint pure olive oil, corn oil
  or ground-nut oil
¼ pint double cream
4 oz. peeled prawns

Cut the melon into six slices, discard the seeds and sprinkle with a little lemon juice, if liked. Place spoonfuls of Prawn mayonnaise into hollows and decorate each slice with two unpeeled prawns.

TO PREPARE MAYONNAISE: Add caster sugar, salt, black pepper and dry mustard to the egg yolk in a bowl. Add the lemon juice and mix thoroughly. Very gradually add the oil, drop by drop, beating well after each addition until all the oil has been used. Lightly whip the cream and fold into the mayonnaise together with the prawns. Check seasoning. Use at once.

Stuffed eggs

SERVES: FOUR

4 hard-boiled eggs
1½ oz. finely grated Cheddar or
  Gruyère cheese
2 teaspoons anchovy essence
1–2 tablespoons mayonnaise
salt and pepper

TO GARNISH:

lettuce or watercress
8 stuffed olives

Cut the eggs in half lengthwise. Remove yolks carefully and beat together with the finely grated Cheddar or Gruyère cheese, and the anchovy essence and mayonnaise. Season to taste. Pile mixture into the egg whites using a teaspoon. Serve two halves per person on individual plates with a little lettuce or watercress; garnish each half with a stuffed olive.

Salmon cream in lemon cups

SERVES: FOUR

2 large lemons
¼ pint double cream
1 can (3½ oz.) salmon
salt and pepper
4 heaped teaspoons chopped
  cucumber or a little shredded
  lettuce
paprika pepper

Cut the lemons in half crosswise. Carefully squeeze out the juice without damaging the skins. Use teaspoon to remove pith, leaving inside of lemon cup smooth. Trim bases of cups so they stand firmly. Whip the cream with 1 tablespoon lemon juice until stiff enough to stand in peaks. Strain the liquid from the can of salmon and turn contents on to a plate, removing any black skin. Mash salmon with a fork and fold it into whipped cream. Season to taste with salt and pepper. Place a teaspoon of chopped cucumber or a little shredded lettuce in each lemon cup. Pile in salmon cream and top with a sprinkling of paprika pepper.

ZIG ZAG MELON

Divide into portions. Remove seeds and loosen flesh

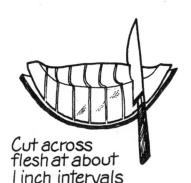

Cut across flesh at about 1 inch intervals

Push sections into zig zag pattern. Decorate with cherry & mint

Taramasalata — Cod's roe pâté

SERVES: SIX

6 oz. smoked cod's roe
10–12 tablespoons olive oil
2 tablespoons lemon juice
freshly ground black pepper
1 level dessertspoon finely
  chopped chives
1 level tablespoon finely chopped
  parsley

TO SERVE:
cocktail biscuits or toast

Remove skin carefully from roe and discard. Place roe in a bowl. Pour 2–3 tablespoons of olive oil over roe and let stand 10 minutes. Pass this mixture through a fine sieve and beat thoroughly until smooth. Add lemon juice and the remaining olive oil, 1 tablespoon at a time. Beat thoroughly after each addition until a soft creamy consistency is formed. Add freshly ground black pepper to taste and mix in the finely chopped chives and parsley. Serve spread on small cocktail biscuits as a cocktail savoury or with freshly made toast as a first course.

Liver pâté

SERVES: SIX TO EIGHT

6 oz. chicken liver
6 oz. calves liver
6 oz. pigs liver
2 oz. lard
6 oz. butter
1 tablespoon brandy
salt and pepper
1 bay leaf
2 oz. finely chopped cooked
  tongue
2 sticks celery
1 lb. loaf of bread

Rinse and dry chicken, calves, and pigs liver then chop finely. Heat lard and 2 oz. of the butter in a saucepan, add livers and cook until brown all over then add brandy, salt and pepper and bay leaf. Cook gently for about 10 minutes. Remove bay leaf then pass mixture through a sieve or liquidizer of an electric food mixer. Beat further 2 oz. butter into the mixture, add finely chopped tongue and scrubbed chopped celery. Allow to cool. Cut a slice from the top of the loaf and scoop out almost all the centre crumb (this can be used for breadcrumbs), spread inside walls of loaf with remaining butter and fill with prepared mixture. Set in refrigerator or cool place for at least 1 hour before serving in slices.

Grilled grapefruit

SERVES: FOUR

2 grapefruit
4 teaspoons sweet sherry
4 tablespoons Demerara sugar
$\frac{1}{2}$ oz. butter

TO GARNISH:
2 maraschino or glacé cherries
mint leaves, if available

Cut the grapefruit in half. Remove pips. Use a sharp knife to cut round fruit and divide into segments (see sketches below). Pour a teaspoon of sweet sherry over each half then sprinkle Demerara sugar liberally over the fruit. Dot with butter. Place under preheated medium grill for 5–10 minutes till heated through. Transfer to individual serving dishes. Top each portion with a halved maraschino or glacé cherry and 2 small mint leaves. Serve immediately.

PREPARING GRAPEFRUIT

Loosen flesh from skin

Divide into segments

Top with cocktail cherry. Serve with sugar

Starters

Tomatoes Monaco
(*Illustrated left*)
SERVES: SIX
6 large firm tomatoes
4 oz. cooked white fish
1 finely chopped hard-boiled egg
1 dessertspoon finely grated onion
2–3 tablespoons mayonnaise
salt and pepper
TO GARNISH:
1 hard-boiled egg
6 black olives
few sprigs of parsley

Cut a slice from top of each tomato and scoop out flesh with a teaspoon. (Set aside and use as a filling for an omelette.) Remove skin and any bones from fish, flake finely and place in bowl with one finely chopped egg. Add grated onion to the fish mixture, bind to a fairly soft consistency with the mayonnaise and season to taste. Divide mixture between tomato cases. Garnish each with a wedge of hard-boiled egg, a black olive, and sprigs of parsley.

These five recipes make a good mixed hors-d'œuvre tray, but each recipe can be used individually, if wished.

Sardines with pimientos
SERVES: TWO
1 can (4½ oz.) sardines
few lettuce leaves
TO GARNISH:
1 can (4 oz.) pimientos

Drain oil from sardines. Arrange lettuce and sardines in serving dish. Drain pimientos and cut into strips and use to garnish.

Hors-d'œuvre eggs
SERVES: FOUR
4 hard-boiled eggs
1 tablespoon single cream or top of the milk
2–3 tablespoons made mayonnaise (see p. 189)
2 tablespoons finely chopped mustard pickles
TO GARNISH:
sliced gherkin

Shell eggs and cut in half. Blend cream or milk with mayonnaise and the finely chopped mustard pickles. Use to coat eggs in serving dish and garnish with slices of gherkin.

Ham and pineapple rice
SERVES: TWO
2 oz. cold cooked long grain rice
2 slices chopped cooked ham
1 small blanched chopped green pepper
1 can (8¾ oz.) crushed pineapple, drained
2 teaspoons finely grated onion
salt and pepper

Mix cold rice, chopped ham, chopped green pepper, crushed drained pineapple and onion together. Season to taste and turn into serving dish.

Tomatoes in sweet and sour dressing
SERVES: TWO
4 large tomatoes
3 dessertspoons wine vinegar
1 teaspoon water
1 rounded teaspoon caster sugar
2 tablespoons finely chopped celery
1 tablespoon finely chopped onion

Skin and slice tomatoes. Place in serving dish. Shake wine vinegar, water, caster sugar, chopped celery and onion together in a screwtop jar until sugar has dissolved, then pour over tomatoes.

Normandy salad
SERVES: TWO
1 cut clove of garlic
pinch salt
black pepper
1 dessertspoon vinegar
3 dessertspoons oil
1 packet (8 oz.) frozen green beans, cooked
1 can (2 oz.) anchovy fillets

Rub bowl with clove of garlic. Place salt, black pepper, vinegar and oil in bowl and mix thoroughly. Add cooked green beans and drained, chopped anchovies. Toss all together and turn into serving dish.

PEELING TOMATOES

Cover with boiling water 1 minute

Drain. Cover with cold water

Strip off skin with small knife

2
Soups

French onion soup (*recipe overleaf*)

Hot soups

French onion soup

SERVES: SIX

1½ lb. onions
4 tablespoons cooking oil
2 oz. butter
1 oz. plain flour
2½ pints stock (made from beef stock cube)
salt and pepper
3 large slices crusty bread
2 oz. Gruyère cheese

Peel and chop onions. Heat the oil and butter in a large pan, add onions and cook very gently until transparent and pale golden in colour. Sprinkle in flour and cook for 1 minute. Add stock, stirring all the time. Bring to the boil and simmer for approximately 50 minutes. Season to taste and pour into a large ovenproof soup tureen or casserole dish. Cut bread slices in half and float on top of soup. Sprinkle with finely grated Gruyère cheese. Place in a preheated hot oven (425 deg. F.—Mark 7) for approximately 10 minutes or place under a preheated grill until cheese is bubbling and golden brown. Serve at once.

Tomato soup

SERVES: FOUR

2 slices streaky bacon
1 small onion
1 small carrot
½ oz. butter
1½ lb. ripe chopped tomatoes
1 pint stock (made from chicken stock cube)
1 teaspoon sugar
1 bouquet garni
salt and pepper
1 oz. cornflour
¼ pint milk
1 dessertspoon tomato purée
¼ pint single cream

Trim the rind from the bacon. Chop bacon into small pieces. Peel and finely chop the onion and carrot. Melt the butter in pan, fry the bacon, onion and carrot together until onion is transparent. Add the washed, chopped tomatoes and fry gently for a few minutes. Pour in the stock, add sugar, bouquet garni and seasoning to taste. Bring to the boil and simmer for approximately 30 minutes. Remove bouquet garni. Pass soup through a fine sieve or liquidizer and return to rinsed pan. Blend the cornflour with a little of the milk and the tomato purée. Stir into the soup together with the remainder of the milk and bring to boil, stirring all the time. Simmer gently for 3–5 minutes. Cool slightly. Stir in cream, check seasoning and serve immediately.

Cream of mushroom soup

SERVES: FOUR

½ lb. mushrooms
¾ pint stock (made from chicken stock cube)
1 small peeled sliced onion
1 oz. butter or margarine
1 oz. plain flour
¾ pint milk
salt and pepper
2 tablespoons cream or top of milk
chopped parsley

Wash and slice the mushrooms. Place in a pan with the stock and peeled and sliced onion. Bring to the boil, cover and simmer for 20–30 minutes till tender. Rub through a sieve or pass through a liquidizer. Melt butter or margarine in a pan, add the flour and cook for 1 minute. Gradually blend in the milk, then the prepared mushroom purée and seasoning to taste. Bring to the boil, stirring, cover and simmer for 5–10 minutes. Just before serving mix in the cream or top of the milk. Sprinkle with chopped parsley.

CROUTONS

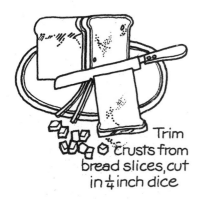

Trim crusts from bread slices, cut in ¼ inch dice

Fry in hot fat until golden and crisp

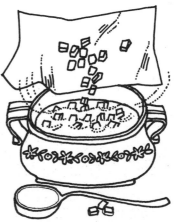

Drain on kitchen paper. Serve with soup

Chicken and leek soup

SERVES: SIX TO EIGHT

6 oz. streaky bacon
2–2½ lb. leeks
3 pints stock (made from chicken stock cube)
1 chicken carcass
¾ pint milk
1½ level tablespoons cornflour
6 oz. finely diced cold cooked chicken
1½ oz. butter
pepper to taste

TO GARNISH:
Chopped grilled streaky bacon

Remove rinds from bacon (reserve rashers for garnish). Trim, wash and slice leeks. Pour stock into a large pan and add bacon rinds and chicken carcass. Bring to the boil, cover and simmer for 1 hour. Strain through a sieve, return stock to pan, stir in sliced leeks and milk. Continue cooking for 20–25 minutes till leeks are tender. Pass soup through a sieve or liquidizer, a little at a time. Return soup to the pan. Blend cornflour with a little water to form a smooth paste. Stir paste into the soup, bring to the boil, boil for 2–3 minutes stirring continuously. Stir in finely diced chicken, butter and pepper to taste. Heat for 10 minutes. Pour soup into a hot tureen, garnish with chopped, grilled streaky bacon.

Minestrone

SERVES: SIX

2 oz. fat bacon
1 large onion
3 sticks celery
8 oz. potatoes
1 large carrot
few green cabbage leaves
2 large tomatoes
2 oz. butter or margarine
3 pints stock (made from chicken stock cube)
2 oz. shell pasta
2 oz. small pasta shapes
2 level teaspoons tomato purée
salt
freshly ground black pepper
1 tablespoon chopped parsley
½ level teaspoon dried sage
2 level tablespoons grated Parmesan cheese

TO SERVE:
Parmesan cheese

Finely chop bacon. Chop peeled onion. Wash celery and cut into small pieces. Peel and dice potatoes and carrot. Shred washed cabbage leaves. Chop tomatoes. Melt butter or margarine in large saucepan. Add bacon, onion, celery and carrot. Cook over gentle heat for 10 minutes, stir occasionally. Stir in potatoes and stock. Bring to the boil, cover and simmer for 1½ hours. Add the cabbage, tomatoes, pasta, tomato purée, salt and black pepper. Simmer for 20 minutes. Stir in the parsley, dried sage and Parmesan cheese just before serving. Serve with extra Parmesan cheese.

Watercress cream soup

SERVES: THREE TO FOUR

4 bunches (8 oz.) watercress
1 oz. butter or margarine
1 pint stock (made from chicken stock cube)
½ oz. cornflour
¼ pint milk
salt
cayenne pepper
2–3 tablespoons single cream

Rinse bunches of watercress in cold water, then, holding each bunch by the stalk end plunge into a bowl of boiling water. Shake, drain thoroughly and discard coarse stalks. Chop watercress. Melt butter or margarine in saucepan. Add chopped watercress and cook gently for 2–3 minutes. Pass through a sieve together with a little of the stock to form a purée. Alternatively, place in a liquidizer. Blend cornflour with a little of the milk to form a smooth paste, then stir in remaining milk and stock. Pour into pan and add watercress purée and seasoning. Reheat slowly in pan, stirring throughout, till soup thickens. Simmer for 3–5 minutes, then remove from heat and cool slightly. Stir in cream and serve.

GARNISHES FOR SOUP

Cream: gently pour into bowls of tomato soup

Parsley: chop heads finely with scissors. Sprinkle on soup.

Bacon: trim and grill until crisp. Crumble over soup

Cold soups

Vichyssoise (Leek and potato soup)

(*Illustrated left*)
SERVES: FOUR TO SIX
2 lb. leeks
8 oz. potatoes
1½ oz. butter
2 pints stock (made from chicken stock cube)
¼ pint cream
salt and pepper
TO SERVE:
1 tablespoon chopped chives, parsley or fresh tarragon

Wash leeks and slice white parts only (use green parts in stews and casseroles). Peel and slice the potatoes. Melt butter in a pan, add leeks and potatoes, cook very slowly for 5–10 minutes without browning. Add stock, bring to boil, cover and simmer gently for 30 minutes till vegetables are very soft. Pass the soup through a sieve or liquidizer. Leave in a bowl to cool, then cover and chill if possible. Just before serving, mix in the cream and seasoning to taste. Serve sprinkled with the chives, parsley or tarragon.

Cream of cucumber soup

SERVES: FOUR
1 large cucumber
1 small onion or shallot
1½ pints stock (made from chicken stock cube)
few sprigs of mint
1 level dessertspoon arrowroot
1 tablespoon milk
salt and pepper
4 tablespoons cream
TO SERVE:
cucumber slices
mint

Peel the cucumber and cut into small pieces. Peel and chop the onion or shallot and place in a pan with the stock. Bring to the boil, cover and simmer for 10–15 minutes. Add the prepared cucumber and mint and cook till tender, about 10–15 minutes. Pass soup through a sieve or liquidizer and return to the pan. Blend the arrowroot with the milk and mix into the pan. Bring to the boil, stirring all the time and cook for ½ minute. Add seasoning to taste and cream. If liked colour lightly with a little green vegetable colouring. Turn soup into bowl, chill thoroughly. Serve in soup bowls topped with thin slices cucumber and mint sprigs.

Gazpacho

SERVES: FOUR TO SIX
1 lb. ripe peeled tomatoes
½ small onion
1 clove of garlic
salt and pepper
2 tablespoons tarragon vinegar
squeeze of lemon juice
3 tablespoons olive oil
1 can (14 oz.) tomato juice
a few cubes crushed ice
a little chopped parsley
TO SERVE:
1 diced green pepper
¼ diced cucumber
3 diced, peeled and seeded tomatoes
bread croûtons (see p. 14)

Press peeled tomatoes through a coarse sieve, discarding seeds; or alternatively, place in a liquidizer to make a purée. Peel and finely grate onion and crush the clove of garlic. Add to the tomato purée with salt, pepper, tarragon vinegar, lemon juice and olive oil. Stir well, then add tomato juice and chill in cool place or refrigerator for at least 1 hour. Add a little crushed ice, if desired, and sprinkle each serving with a little chopped parsley. Serve with green pepper, cucumber, tomatoes and croûtons.

USEFUL EQUIPMENT

Nylon sieve–
for fine purée of vegetables or fruit

Electric liquidizer–to chop vegetables, make purees and sauces

Garlic Press–
for pressing garlic to to obtain pulp and juices

3
Fish

Sea-water
Smoked
River
Shell
Chef's specials
Menus

Grilled halibut (*recipe overleaf*)

Sea-water fish

Grilled halibut

SERVES: FOUR

4 halibut cutlets (approximately 6–8 oz. each)
salt and pepper
2–3 oz. butter
1 tablespoon salad oil
1 can (11½ oz.) sweetcorn with red and green peppers

TO GARNISH:
a little canned pimiento
few sprigs of parsley
lemon wedges

Wipe halibut cutlets with a damp cloth. Sprinkle each side with salt and pepper. Heat butter in grill pan together with salad oil. Place cutlets into hot fat and brush tops with melted fat. Cook for 10–15 minutes till the fish is golden brown and cooked through. Brush with melted fat occasionally during cooking. Heat sweetcorn in a saucepan. Cut drained pimiento into neat strips. Place drained sweetcorn in centre of a hot dish and arrange halibut on either side. Garnish sweetcorn with strips of pimiento and fish with sprigs of parsley. Serve with lemon wedges.

Fried fish in batter

SERVES: SIX

6 haddock fillets or tail ends cod
deep fat for frying

BATTER:
6 oz. plain flour
¼ teaspoon salt
3 dessertspoons cooking oil
approximately 7 fl. oz. tepid water
2 egg whites

Wash and dry haddock fillets or tail ends cod thoroughly on absorbent paper. Dip fish in prepared batter to coat evenly and hold over bowl for a few seconds to allow excess batter to drain away. Place immediately into deep hot fat and fry for about 5 minutes or until golden and cooked through.

TO PREPARE BATTER: Sift flour and salt into a mixing bowl. Make a well in the centre with the back of a wooden spoon. Add oil and half the tepid water. Stir with wooden spoon, gradually drawing in the flour from the sides of the bowl. Add a little more of the water and beat well to a coating consistency. Whisk egg whites until stiff. Fold into batter with a metal spoon and use straight away.

Florentine plaice

SERVES: THREE

6 plaice fillets
salt
freshly ground black pepper
strained juice of ½ lemon
2 tablespoons water
1 packet (8 oz.) frozen leaf spinach
½ pint freshly made thick white sauce (see p. 186)
2–3 oz. finely grated Gruyère cheese

Remove the skin from the plaice fillets with a sharp knife, fold each fillet in half, skinned side inside. Transfer fish to an ovenproof dish and sprinkle well with seasoning. Pour lemon juice and water over. Cover with a lid or kitchen foil and bake in the centre of a moderately hot oven (375 deg. F. —Mark 5) for approximately 15 minutes or until fish is tender and cooked through. Cook leaf spinach according to packet directions. Strain liquid from fish into white sauce and stir well together. Arrange spinach on top of fish, then cover with prepared sauce. Sprinkle with grated Gruyère cheese and return to oven for 15–20 minutes until golden brown and well heated through. There is no need to serve this dish with any extra vegetables, but freshly cooked potatoes would be an ideal accompaniment.

LEMON BUTTERFLIES

Remove pips from thin lemon slices, cut in half

Cut through rind to centre of each slice

Gently pull into wings without separating

Savoury whiting

SERVES: FOUR
4 fillets whiting
4 oz. curd or cream cheese
salt
a little paprika pepper
8 oz. ribbon noodles
2 oz. button mushrooms
1½–2 oz. butter
1 packet (5 oz.) frozen peas, cooked

TO GARNISH:
slices of lemon
sprigs of parsley

Rinse fish and pat dry. Spread top of each fillet with curd or cream cheese then sprinkle with salt and paprika pepper. Place in base of grill pan and cook under medium heat for 8–10 minutes or until cooked through. Cook ribbon noodles in boiling salted water until tender (see packet directions). Drain well through colander and pour boiling water over to keep noodles from sticking. Rinse, dry and slice button mushrooms. Fry in melted butter in large pan until tender, 3–5 minutes. Add drained noodles and cooked peas. Stir over medium heat until warmed through. Turn on to serving platter and arrange cooked fish on top. Garnish with slices of lemon and sprigs of parsley.

Mackerel in parcels

SERVES: FOUR
4 mackerel (approximately 8 oz. each)
3 oz. butter or margarine
1 small grated onion
1 teaspoon made mustard
1 teaspoon lemon juice
salt and pepper
4 small bay leaves
few capers or stuffed olives

TO GARNISH:
lemon wedges
parsley

Rinse and wipe mackerel. Clean and remove tails, fins and eyes but leave on heads. Cream 2 oz. of the butter or margarine, add grated onion, mustard and lemon juice. Beat well, add salt and pepper. Spread mixture into the belly cavity of each fish. Place each fish on a piece of kitchen foil and brush with remaining melted butter or margarine. Place bay leaf on each fish, then form into four parcels, sealing the foil ends so the fish will cook in their own juices. Bake in a moderately hot oven (375 deg. F.—Mark 5) for 30–35 minutes or until fish are cooked through. Serve individually in parcels, with the foil folded back, or arrange the fish on a platter. Remove bay leaf from each parcel and set a few capers or a half stuffed olive in position for eye. Garnish with lemon wedges and parsley.

Cod Portuguese

SERVES: FOUR
1–2 oz. butter
8 oz. boiled sliced potatoes
1 chopped onion
8 oz. quartered tomatoes
pinch lemon thyme
4 cod steaks (½ inch thick)
salt and pepper
juice of ½ lemon
4 tablespoons cider
parsley

Butter shallow ovenproof dish with a little of the butter (keep remainder for cooking), cover base with boiled, sliced potatoes and chopped onion. Add quartered tomatoes and sprinkle with lemon thyme. Lay cod on vegetables. season, sprinkle with lemon juice, moisten with cider. Dot fish with butter, cover and bake in a hot oven (400 deg. F.—Mark 6) for 45–50 minutes. Sprinkle with parsley.

LEMON TWISTS

Cut lemon into very thin slices

Cut slice from centre to outer edge

Twist ends in opposite directions

Sea-water fish

Soused herrings

(*Illustrated left*)

SERVES: FIVE

5 herrings
salt and black pepper
¼ pint malt vinegar
¼ pint water
¼ teaspoon pickling spice
2 bay leaves
1 small onion

TO SERVE:

Mustard sauce (see p. 188)
bread and butter

Remove herring heads with knife or scissors and discard. Scrape each herring from tail to head with back of knife to remove scales. Slit fish along underside to tail and remove roe and blood-vessels. Open each fish and place cut side down on board. Press firmly along centre backbone to flatten fish. Turn over and remove backbone. Trim tail and fins with scissors. Rinse and pat dry on cloth or absorbent paper. Sprinkle with salt and black pepper. Roll up from tail to head and place close together in an ovenproof dish. Pour over malt vinegar and water and sprinkle with pickling spice. Add bay leaves. Peel onion, slice into rings, add to dish. Cover with lid or foil and bake in a very slow oven (275 deg. F.—Mark 1) for 1½ hours. Leave to cool in liquid in dish. Serve cold, with Mustard sauce, bread and butter.

Curried fish

SERVES: THREE TO FOUR

8–12 oz. cooked white fish

CURRY SAUCE:

1 onion
1 clove of garlic
2 tablespoons corn oil
1 level tablespoon curry powder
1 level teaspoon curry paste
1 oz. cornflour
¾ pint stock or water
1 finely chopped cored apple
1 dessertspoon redcurrant jelly
juice of ½ lemon
1 tablespoon sultanas
2 level tablespoons desiccated coconut soaked in 3 tablespoons boiling water

TO SERVE:

12 oz. freshly boiled rice

Cut the fish into small pieces and add to freshly prepared curry sauce. Cook gently for 5 minutes or until well heated through, then serve on bed of freshly boiled rice.

TO PREPARE SAUCE: Peel and chop onion and clove of garlic and fry gently in corn oil until tender. Stir in the curry powder, curry paste and cornflour. Cook over gentle heat, stirring, for 2–3 minutes. Gradually blend in stock or water, then add finely chopped cored apple, redcurrant jelly, lemon juice and sultanas. Stir until boiling then simmer 45 minutes. Add strained coconut liquor.

Simon's pie

SERVES: FOUR

8 oz. plain flour
pinch of salt
pinch of cayenne pepper
¼ level teaspoon dry mustard
4 oz. margarine
3 oz. finely grated Cheddar cheese
1 egg yolk
2–3 tablespoons cold water
a little milk to glaze

FILLING:

1 lb. cooked fresh haddock
1 can (10 oz.) condensed cream of mushroom soup
¼ pint milk
salt and pepper

TO PREPARE PASTRY: Sift flour, salt, cayenne pepper and dry mustard into mixing bowl. Rub in margarine with fingers until mixture resembles fine breadcrumbs. Stir in Cheddar cheese then mix into a firm dough with egg yolk beaten with cold water

TO PREPARE FILLING: Skin and flake haddock, removing bones. Blend soup with milk, mix in fish. Season to taste. Turn into a 1½-pint pie dish. Damp edges of dish, press pastry into position over filling. Trim off surplus pastry then knock up and decorate edges. Brush over top with little milk. Make a small hole in centre of pie. Bake just above centre in hot oven (400 deg. F.–Mark 6) for 35–40 minutes.

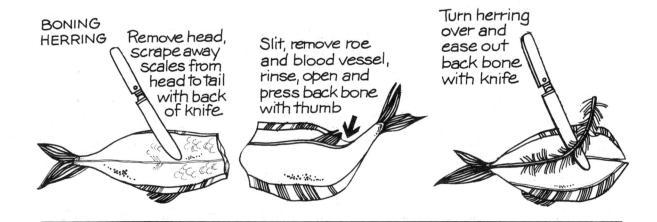

BONING HERRING — Remove head, scrape away scales from head to tail with back of knife

Slit, remove roe and blood vessel, rinse, open and press back bone with thumb

Turn herring over and ease out back bone with knife

Smoked fish

Finnan fish cakes
(*Illustrated left*)
MAKES: EIGHT
1 lb. freshly cooked Finnan
   haddock
1 hard-boiled egg
1 oz. butter
8 oz. mashed potatoes
freshly ground black pepper
milk to bind if necessary
1 beaten egg
3 oz. browned breadcrumbs
2 oz. fat
TO GARNISH:
sprigs of parsley

Flake haddock with a knife, removing any skin and bones. Chop
fish coarsely. Chop hard-boiled
egg. Melt butter in a saucepan.
Add the fish, hard-boiled egg,
potatoes, black pepper to taste,
and a little milk to bind if necessary. Stir well then turn mixture
out on to a plate and allow to cool.
Shape cold mixture into eight neat
flat round shapes on a lightly
floured board. Dip in beaten egg
and coat with breadcrumbs. Fry
in hot shallow melted fat for 5
minutes on each side, till golden
brown. Drain on soft kitchen
paper. Transfer to a serving dish
and garnish with sprigs of parsley.

Kipper pâté
SERVES: EIGHT
1 packet (8 oz.) frozen boneless
   kipper fillets
4 oz. melted butter
strained juice of $\frac{1}{2}$ lemon
5 tablespoons double cream,
   whipped
black pepper
TO GARNISH:
slice of lemon
sprigs of parsley
TO SERVE:
Melba toast

Allow kipper fillets to thaw.
Gently cook the kipper fillets in
half the melted butter until soft,
then pass through a fine mincer
or a sieve or liquidizer. Add remaining melted butter to the
kipper purée. Mix in the lemon
juice, whipped cream and pepper
to taste. Turn into serving bowl
and leave in a cool place to chill.
Garnish with lemon and sprigs of
parsley. Serve with Melba toast.

Fisherman's breakfast
SERVES: ONE
4–6 oz. portion smoked haddock
   fillet
1–2 oz. butter
2 rashers bacon
$\frac{1}{2}$ oz. cooking fat
1 egg
salt and pepper
TO GARNISH:
sprig of parsley
TO SERVE:
hot soft roll or toast

Wipe haddock, dot with butter
and cook in base of grill pan under
medium heat until cooked through.
Baste with butter whilst cooking
to keep fish moist. Trim rind
from bacon rashers, place bacon
on grill-pan rack. Cook on both
sides until crisp. Melt fat in frying
pan and drop in egg. Sprinkle
with salt and pepper. Fry until
cooked according to taste. Serve
haddock, bacon and egg on
warmed serving plate. Garnish
with parsley and serve with a hot
soft roll or toast.

COATING IN
EGG AND BREADCRUMBS

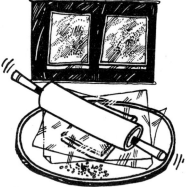

Bake stale bread till
golden. Crush with
rolling pin

Dip fishcakes or
fish in beaten egg

Coat in browned crumbs
on greaseproof paper

River fish

Trout with almonds

(*Illustrated left*)

SERVES: FOUR

4 trout
1 tablespoon seasoned flour
3 oz. butter
2–3 oz. flaked or chopped
    almonds
2 tablespoons lemon juice
1 tablespoon chopped parsley
TO SERVE:
freshly cooked vegetables

Ask the fishmonger to gut the trout. Wipe the fish with a clean damp cloth then toss in seasoned flour. Melt 1 oz. butter in frying pan. Add the almonds, fry until lightly browned, then remove from pan and keep on one side. Add remaining butter to pan and fry the trout gently, turning once during the cooking until nicely browned and cooked through, about 10 minutes. Sprinkle with the browned almonds, lemon juice and chopped parsley. Transfer to a serving dish and serve with freshly cooked vegetables.

Cold salmon

SERVES: EIGHT TO TEN

1 large piece (2½ lb.) fresh
    salmon
1 small onion
2 small carrots
1 pint slightly salted water
3 parsley stalks
1 bay leaf
1 sprig of thyme
6 peppercorns
½ glass (2 fl. oz.) white wine
2 tablespoons wine vinegar
TO SERVE:
lettuce
cucumber slices
radish roses
tomato halves

Remove any scales from salmon, scraping with back of knife from tail end. Rinse well, removing all the blood. Peel and slice onion and carrots and cut into ¼-inch slices. Place prepared vegetables into a large saucepan with salted water, parsley stalks, bay leaf, sprig of thyme and peppercorns. Allow to come to the boil and boil for 20 minutes, then add white wine and wine vinegar and lower in the fish. Cover and boil gently. Allow 10 minutes to the lb. and 10 minutes over. When cooked for the appropriate time remove from heat and leave to cool for 5 minutes then carefully lift from pan and drain well. Remove skin and any dark flesh. Leave to become completely cold. Serve on platter on a bed of lettuce garnished with cucumber slices, radish roses and tomato halves.

Grilled salmon steaks

SERVES: TWO

2 salmon steaks (middle cut, ½–¾
    inch thick)
salt
freshly ground black pepper
2 oz. butter
TO SERVE:
MAÎTRE d'HÔTEL BUTTER:
2 oz. butter
2 teaspoons strained lemon juice
1 tablespoon finely chopped
    parsley
½ lemon
salt and pinch of cayenne pepper
TO GARNISH:
lemon wedges

Wipe salmon steaks with clean damp cloth then sprinkle with salt and freshly ground black pepper. Set aside and prepare Maître d'Hôtel butter (see the sketches below). Place salmon steaks in base of a lightly buttered grill pan and dot fish with remaining butter. Place under hot grill and grill for 4 minutes, then turn and cook for further 3–6 minutes or until steaks are cooked through. Serve immediately with Maître d'Hôtel butter and garnish with lemon wedges.

MAITRE D'HOTEL BUTTER

Work two teaspoons strained lemon juice into 2oz butter

Add pinch cayenne pepper, 1 tablespoon chopped parsley

Form into roll, chill till firm. Cut into pats

Shell fish

Seafood cocktail

(*Illustrated left*)

SERVES: SIX TO EIGHT

8 oz. fresh or frozen prawns
1 can (6 oz.) crab or lobster
   meat
1 can (4½ oz.) mussels
freshly ground pepper
juice of ½ lemon
2 sliced hard-boiled eggs
3 sliced tomatoes
TOMATO MAYONNAISE:
8 tablespoons mayonnaise
2 tablespoons single cream
1–2 teaspoons tomato purée
salt and pepper
TO GARNISH:
3 slices of smoked salmon
slices of lemon

If the prawns are frozen allow to thaw as directed on packet. Drain the liquid from the crab or lobster and divide meat into pieces. Drain the mussels. Mix the prepared fish together with the ground pepper and lemon juice. Place slices of egg in six-to-eight individual dishes, arrange slices of tomato round the edge and pile the fish mixture in the centre. Coat with 1 dessertspoon of tomato mayonnaise and garnish with a roll of smoked salmon and half a slice of lemon. Serve remainder of mayonnaise in a separate dish.
TO PREPARE THE TOMATO MAYONNAISE: Blend mayonnaise, cream, purée together, season to taste.

Shrimp croquettes

MAKES: APPROXIMATELY TWELVE

2 oz. butter or margarine
2 oz. plain flour
¾ pint milk
½ oz. gelatine
juice of ½ lemon
a good pinch of nutmeg and
   cayenne pepper
salt
1 beaten egg yolk
8 oz. peeled shrimps or prawns
TO COAT:
2 large eggs and 1 egg white
approximately 10 tablespoons
   browned breadcrumbs
deep fat or oil for frying
TO SERVE:
lemon
fried parsley (see p. 155)

Melt butter or margarine in a pan, stir in the flour and cook for 1 minute. Blend in milk gradually, bring to boil and cook, stirring for 2 minutes. Dissolve gelatine in lemon juice and add to mixture together with nutmeg, cayenne pepper and salt to taste. Remove from heat and add beaten egg yolk and chopped shrimps or prawns. Turn into an oblong tin about 6 by 9 by 1 inches and allow to set firmly, overnight if possible. Cut into squares and coat with beaten eggs and egg white then breadcrumbs. Coat a second time with remaining egg and breadcrumbs to give a thick coating. Fry in hot deep fat or oil till golden. Drain well and serve with lemon and fried parsley.

Scallops au gratin

SERVES: FOUR

4 scallops (keep the shells to
   serve scallops in)
½ pint milk
salt and pepper
½ oz. butter
½ oz. flour
2 oz. grated Cheddar cheese
2–3 tablespoons fresh white
   breadcrumbs

Wash scallops well under running cold water. Cut into neat pieces. Place in a saucepan. Cover with milk, season to taste. Bring to the boil, reduce heat and simmer for 8 minutes until tender. Strain off milk into a jug. Transfer scallops to a plate. Melt butter in a saucepan. Stir in flour and cook gently for ½ minute. Remove from heat and gradually blend in strained milk. Bring to boil, stirring, and boil for 2–3 minutes. Add grated Cheddar cheese and scallops, simmer for a few minutes until cheese is melted and scallops are heated through. Divide the mixture between the well-washed shells. Sprinkle breadcrumbs on each scallop. Cook under a preheated grill for a few minutes till golden brown. Serve immediately.

SHELL FISH SEASONS

Prawns: seasonable
all year, best
February–October

Scallops: seasonable
November–March, best
January and February

Shrimps: seasonable
April–September

Shell fish

Crab salad
(*Illustrated left*)

SERVES: SIX
8 oz. cooked crab meat
strained juice of ½ lemon
salt
freshly ground black pepper
6 small lettuce leaves
6 freshly made small squares of
    toast
TOPPING:
1 oz. butter
2 eggs
2 tablespoons milk
salt and pepper
1 tablespoon mayonnaise
1 finely chopped hard-boiled egg

Reserve a little of the crab meat for garnish. Flake remainder of crab then moisten with strained lemon juice and season with salt and freshly ground black pepper. Arrange lettuce leaves on the toast. Place spoonfuls of the crab on the lettuce then top with prepared topping and garnish with remainder of crab.

TO PREPARE TOPPING: Melt butter in pan then whisk eggs, milk and seasoning lightly together. Pour into pan and stir gently until egg mixture lightly sets. Allow to cool. Stir in mayonnaise and finely chopped hard-boiled egg.

Egg and prawn toppers

SERVES: FOUR
1 oz. butter or margarine
1 oz. plain flour
½ pint milk
salt and pepper
1 tablespoon lemon juice
1 teaspoon anchovy essence
1 pint (about 12 oz.) whole
    prawns
1 tablespoon finely chopped
    chives
4 thick slices bread
oil for frying
2 halved hard-boiled eggs

Melt the butter or margarine in a saucepan, sprinkle in the flour and stir over gentle heat for 1 minute. Remove from heat and gradually blend in the milk. Return to heat, bring to boil and simmer 2–3 minutes, stirring throughout to form a smooth thick sauce. Season to taste, then stir in lemon juice and anchovy essence. Peel prawns. Keep sixteen whole then chop the rest and add to the prepared sauce together with 1 level tablespoon chopped chives. Fry the bread slices in hot oil until golden brown and crisp on both sides, then drain well on kitchen paper. Reheat the prawn sauce if necessary then place on top of the prepared fried bread. Arrange halved hard-boiled eggs on top then decorate with whole prawns. Serve hot.

Simple lobster thermidor

SERVES: TWO
1 cooked lobster (2½ lb.)
½ pint prepared Béchamel sauce
    (see p. 186)
2 tablespoons double cream
squeeze of lemon juice
1 tablespoon dry sherry
¼ level teaspoon dry mustard
dash Worcester sauce
pinch of cayenne pepper
¼ level teaspoon salt
freshly ground black pepper
1 oz. finely grated Parmesan
    cheese
little paprika pepper
1 oz. butter
TO SERVE:
lemon wedges

Cut lobster in half lengthwise. Follow steps 1, 2 and 3 of 'Dressing a lobster' (see p. 199). Cut into large cubes. Reserve shells for serving. Gently heat prepared Béchamel sauce, add cream and allow sauce to become hot without boiling. Stir in lemon juice, dry sherry, dry mustard, Worcester sauce and cayenne pepper. Season with salt and freshly ground black pepper. Add lobster meat and heat through. Pile into lobster shells, sprinkle with Parmesan cheese and a little paprika pepper. Dot with butter and brown under a hot grill for 1 minute. Serve at once with lemon wedges.

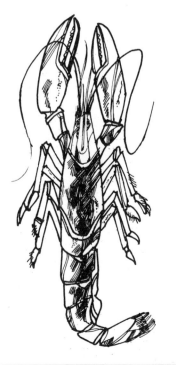

SHELL FISH SEASONS

Lobster
Seasonable March –
November, but
available most of
the year

Crab
Seasonable
April – October

Chef's special

Sole with mushrooms
(*Illustrated left*)

SERVES: THREE
6 sole fillets
salt and pepper
$\frac{1}{2}$ oz. butter
4 oz. button mushrooms
$\frac{1}{4}$ pint milk
SAUCE:
1 oz. margarine or butter
1 oz. flour
$\frac{1}{4}$ pint milk
2 oz. grated cheese
salt
black pepper
pinch of dry mustard
$\frac{1}{4}$ pint single cream
chopped parsley

Skin the fillets, season well with the salt and pepper. Roll up from the tail end and place in a buttered ovenproof dish, together with washed and dried button mushrooms. Pour $\frac{1}{4}$ pint milk over, cover with lid or tin foil. Bake in a moderate oven (350 deg. F.—Mark 4) for about 15 minutes or until cooked through. Remove fish, place on serving dish and keep warm. Pour liquid from cooked fish into jug and reserve for sauce. Keep mushrooms on one side. TO PREPARE SAUCE: Melt the fat in pan, stir in flour, remove from the heat and gradually beat in liquid strained from fish together with the $\frac{1}{4}$ pint of milk. Return to the heat, bring to the boil stirring all the time, add the drained mushrooms, simmer gently for 2 minutes. Remove from the heat, add grated cheese, seasoning to taste, dry mustard and cream. Use immediately. Pour the sauce over the fillets and sprinkle with chopped parsley.

VARIATIONS
This dish can be the basis of many others. The following are particularly good.

1. Omit the mushrooms and add 4 oz. peeled prawns and 1 level teaspoon of paprika pepper to the prepared sauce. Heat through gently before pouring over the fish. Garnish with lemon wedges dipped in paprika pepper.

2. Omit mushrooms, increase the amount of cheese to 4 oz. (a finely grated Parmesan cheese is ideal). Serve fish coated with cheese sauce and garnished with canned asparagus tips which have been heated through and drained.

3. Omit mushrooms. Peel four tomatoes, discard seeds and chop flesh into small pieces. Add to sauce together with 1 level tablespoon finely chopped parsley.

Grilled grapefruit
page 9

☐

Sole with mushrooms
Creamed potatoes
Watercress

☐

Meringues Chantilly
page 125

Suggested wine for main course:
Pouilly Fuissé

SKINNING FILLETS OF FISH

Hold fish at tail end . . . salt ensures a firm grip

Cut with knife, sliding closely to skin

Roll up fillet towards tail-end

Chef's special

Arroz con gambas (Rice with prawns)
(*Illustrated left*)

SERVES: SIX

2 cloves of garlic
2 medium-sized onions
4 tablespoons olive oil
8 large tomatoes
$1\frac{1}{2}$ lb. Valencia rice
a good pinch powdered saffron
$1\frac{1}{4}$–$1\frac{1}{2}$ pints of chicken stock
   (made from chicken stock
   cube)
8 oz. peeled prawns
6 oz. shelled peas (or small
   packet frozen)
6 oz. sliced fresh French beans
   (or small packet frozen)
salt and pepper

TO GARNISH:
lemon wedges
4–6 Pacific or large prawns

Peel and chop garlic and onions. Heat 3 tablespoons of the olive oil in a very large frying pan or saucepan and fry the prepared garlic and onion for about 5 minutes until tender and pale golden brown. Blanch, peel and chop the tomatoes then add to the other ingredients in pan. Stir well and cook for 3–4 minutes. Stir in the Valencia rice and powdered saffron and cook gently, stirring for 5 minutes. Pour the prepared stock into the pan, stir well and cook for 10 minutes. Fry the peeled prawns separately in remaining olive oil for 2–3 minutes until lightly browned. Add to the rice together with the raw or defrosted peas and the sliced or defrosted beans. Cook quickly, stirring for 5 minutes then reduce heat and simmer gently for 10–15 minutes until the rice has absorbed the stock and is tender but the grains are still quite separate. A little more stock can be added during the cooking if necessary. Season to taste. Remove from heat, garnish with lemon wedges and prawns.

VARIATION:
To make this dish into a simple Paella the following ingredients can be added about 10 minutes before the end of cooking time:
1 medium chicken, cut into twelve pieces and gently fried in olive oil for about 12–15 minutes until cooked through
6 oz. bacon or lean pork, cut into small cubes and fried in the oil remaining from the chicken
1 level teaspoon paprika pepper
1 can ($4\frac{1}{2}$ oz.) mussels, well drained

Melon

□

Arroz con gambas
Green salad
page 98

□

Chocolate mousse
page 117

Suggested wine for main course:
Rioja

PEELING PRAWNS

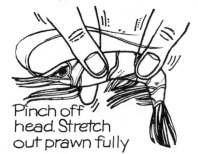

Pinch off head. Stretch out prawn fully

Pinch off tail shell between finger and thumb

Remove body shell and any roe using thumb and forefinger

Fish menus

Ham and pineapple rice
page 11

□

Mackerel in parcels
page 21

Buttered peas

New potatoes

□

Caramel custard
page 115

Tomato soup
page 14

□

Simon's pie
page 23

Simple salad
page 98

□

Winter fruit salad
page 111

**Tomatoes in
sweet and sour dressing**
page 11

□

Grilled halibut
page 20

Creamed potatoes

□

Country house pear pie
page 107

Normandy salad
page 11

□

Simple lobster thermidor
page 31

Green salad
page 98

Buttered new potatoes

□

Lemon meringue pie
page 123

Cream of cucumber soup
page 17

□

Grilled salmon steaks
page 27

Buttered peas

Potato croquettes
page 90

□

**Strawberry and almond
shortcake**
page 119

Watercress cream soup
page 15

□

Trout with almonds
page 27

New potatoes

Green salad
page 98

□

French apple tart
page 121

Hors d'œuvre eggs
page 11

□

Cod Portuguese
page 21

Boiled potatoes

□

Sunset apples
page 113

Apple avocado special
page 101

□

Savoury whiting
page 21

Spinach

□

Lemon meringue pie
page 123

Grilled grapefruit
page 9

☐

Florentine plaice
page 20
Creamy mashed potatoes

☐

Treacle tart
page 107

Italian tomato cocktail
page 182

☐

Scallops au gratin
page 29

Spinach

Potato croquettes
page 90

☐

Coffee party mousse
page 117

Watercress cream soup
page 15

☐

Cold salmon
page 27
New potatoes
Green salad
page 98

☐

**Melon with
rich vanilla ice cream**
page 117

Grilled grapefruit
page 9

☐

Curried fish
page 23
Rice
Sliced banana
Sliced tomato
Mango chutney

☐

Lemon sorbet
page 119

Apple avocado special
page 101

☐

Florentine plaice
page 20
Creamed potatoes

☐

Ice cream

Stuffed eggs
page 8

☐

Curried fish
page 23

Freshly boiled rice
page 49—sketch

☐

Winter fruit salad
page 111

Cream of cucumber soup
page 17

☐

Soused herrings
page 23
Mustard sauce
page 188
Brown bread and butter
Green salad
page 98

☐

Fiesta pancakes
page 106

Sunshine salad
page 98

☐

Fried fish in batter
page 20

Chips

☐

Caramel custard
page 115

4
Meat

Roasts
Fries and grills
Stews and casseroles
Mince
Pies and puddings
Cold meat
Chef's specials
Menus

Roast lamb continental style (*recipe overleaf*)

Roasts

Roast lamb continental style

1 leg of lamb (approximately 3½ lb.)
4 cloves of garlic
3 tablespoons oil or melted cooking fat
salt
TO SERVE:
Mint sauce (see p. 188)

Wipe the joint with a damp cloth then make small incisions with point of sharp small knife into the joint at even intervals. Peel the garlic, and cut each clove into four narrow strips lengthwise and insert in the cuts, pressing in firmly. Place the joint in a roasting tin, add the oil or melted fat and sprinkle with a little salt. Cook in a moderately hot oven (375 deg. F. —Mark 5) allowing 30 minutes to the lb. cooking time. Baste joint from time to time as necessary. Serve on a carving dish or board.

Roast sirloin of beef with Yorkshire puddings

4–5 lb. boned and rolled sirloin of beef
salt
4 oz. dripping or lard
INDIVIDUAL YORKSHIRE PUDDINGS:
4 oz. plain flour
¼ level teaspoon salt
1 egg
½ pint milk
2–3 tablespoons dripping

Weigh the joint and calculate the cooking time and allow 15 minutes to the lb. plus 15 minutes for rare or underdone meat, or allow 20 minutes to the lb. plus 20 minutes for medium. Wipe joint with a clean damp cloth and sprinkle with a little salt. Place in a meat tin and dot with the dripping or lard. Cook in a hot oven (425 deg. F.—Mark 7) for the calculated cooking time.

TO PREPARE YORKSHIRE PUDDINGS: Sift flour and salt into a bowl. Make a well in the centre and break in egg plus 2 tablespoons milk. Beat with wooden spoon gradually drawing in the flour. Add just over half the milk a little at a time, beating well till smooth. Gradually stir in remaining milk. Cover and leave in cool place for 30 minutes. Heat little dripping in small deep patty tins till hot. Half-fill tins with batter, place on shelf above meat for about 15 minutes till risen and golden.

Savoury roast pork

1 small leg of boned pork
1 tablespoon olive oil
salt
STUFFING:
1 lb. onions
4 oz. fresh white breadcrumbs
1 oz. melted butter
2 rounded teaspoons dried sage
salt and pepper
TO SERVE:
Apple sauce (see p. 188)

Wipe the joint with a damp cloth. Stuff the cavity with the prepared stuffing and tie the joint up firmly. Rub the olive oil and then the salt into the skin. Put joint in a meat tin, place on rack and roast in a moderately hot oven (375 deg. F.—Mark 5) for 35 minutes to the lb. (weighed with stuffing) and 30 minutes over.

TO MAKE THE STUFFING: Peel and cut the onions in half. Place in boiling salted water and cook gently for 15 minutes. Drain well then chop finely. Mix with the breadcrumbs, melted butter, sage, salt and pepper to taste.

THICKENED GRAVY

Pour off all but 2 tablespoons fat from tin

Blend in 2 level tablespoons flour

FLOUR

Add stockcube and 1 pint water. Boil for 3 minutes, stirring. Add browning

Apricot stuffed lamb

1 boned breast of lamb
1 oz. lard
STUFFING:
4 oz. dried apricots (soaked overnight)
1 small onion
8 oz. pork sausagemeat
2 oz. fresh white breadcrumbs
1 tablespoon chopped parsley
salt and pepper

Wipe and trim meat, and lay skin side down on board. Spread prepared stuffing evenly over the surface and roll up very firmly. Fasten securely with string. Stand meat in tin with lard on top. Roast in a moderately hot oven (375 deg. F.—Mark 5) 1–1½ hours according to size of joint.
TO PREPARE STUFFING: Drain the apricots and cut into small pieces. Peel and chop onion finely. Mix all ingredients well together.

Stuffed pork chops

SERVES: FOUR
4 thick loin pork chops
salt
TO GARNISH:
few slices of lemon
sprigs of parsley
STUFFING:
1 oz. prunes (soaked overnight in cold water)
1½ oz. fresh white breadcrumbs
1½ oz. chopped salted peanuts
½ level teaspoon salt
freshly ground black pepper
finely grated rind and juice of ½ lemon
a little beaten egg

Wipe and trim the chops. Using a sharp pointed knife, make a cut through centre of each chop to the bone to form a pocket for the stuffing. Press prepared stuffing into each cavity. Sprinkle meat with a little salt and arrange in meat tin, then cook on shelf above centre of moderately hot oven (375 deg. F.—Mark 5) 40–45 minutes. Arrange on serving plate, garnish with lemon and parsley.
TO PREPARE STUFFING: Remove stones from prunes, cut flesh in small pieces. Mix with the breadcrumbs, chopped salted peanuts, salt, black pepper, lemon rind and juice and sufficient beaten egg to bind mixture.

Baked forehock with pineapple and sweetcorn

1 forehock (approximately 5 lb.)
8 peppercorns
2 bay leaves
whole cloves
GLAZE:
4 tablespoons golden syrup
4 tablespoons juice from canned pineapple
TO SERVE:
1 can (10½ oz.) pineapple rings, heated
1 packet (8 oz.) frozen sweetcorn, cooked
a few stuffed olives

Soak the forehock overnight in cold water to cover. Drain, then weigh and calculate the cooking time, allowing 25 minutes to the lb. and 25 minutes over. Place the joint in a large saucepan of fresh cold water to cover, add peppercorns and bay leaves. Bring to boil, simmer gently for half calculated cooking time. Remove joint from pan. Carefully strip off skin, score fat and stud with cloves (see sketches below). Place in tin and coat with golden syrup and pineapple juice mixed together. Cover with kitchen foil. Bake in a moderately hot oven (375 deg. F.—Mark 5) for remainder of cooking time, folding back foil and basting with glaze 20 minutes before end of cooking time. Serve with heated pineapple rings, cooked sweetcorn and stuffed olives.

TRIMMING A HAM JOINT

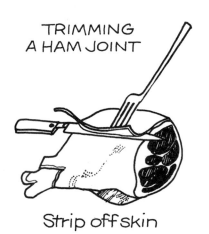

Strip off skin

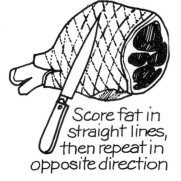

Score fat in straight lines, then repeat in opposite direction

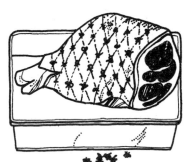

Stud each triangle formed with a clove

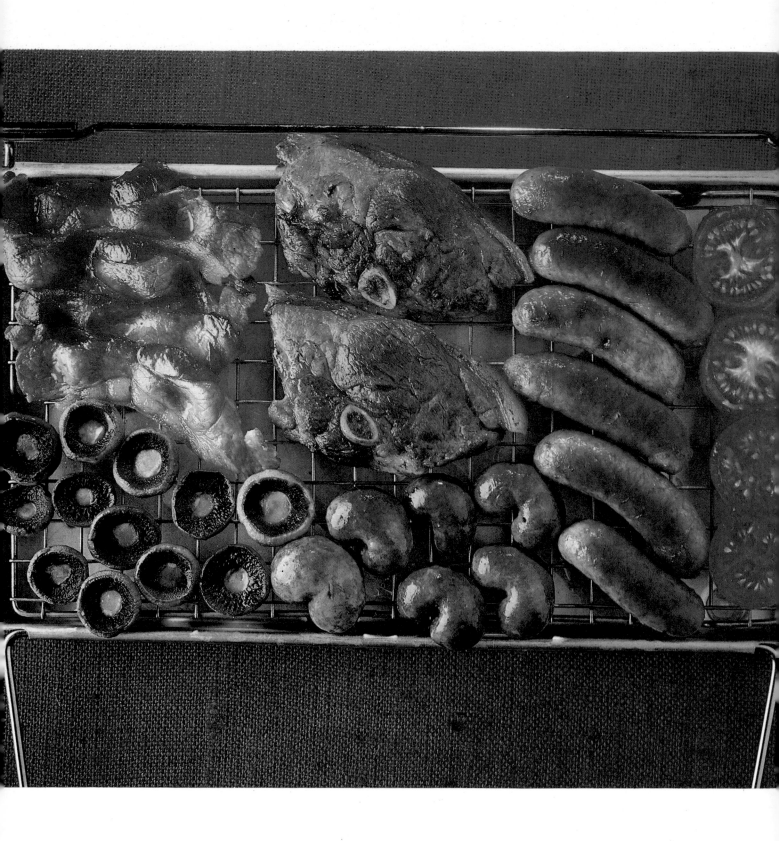

Fries and grills

Mixed grill

(*Illustrated left*)

SERVES: TWO

2 lamb chump chops
3 lambs kidneys
6 pork sausages
4 rashers bacon
cooking oil
salt and pepper
4 oz. rinsed mushrooms
2 halved tomatoes

TO GARNISH:

watercress
potato crisps

Wipe and trim chops, prepare kidneys (see sketches below). Separate sausages. Trim rind from bacon. Place chump chops, kidneys and sausages on grill-pan rack. Brush with oil and sprinkle with salt and pepper. Cook in highest position under preheated hot grill for 1 minute each side to seal juices. Reduce heat to medium. Place rinsed mushrooms and tomato halves in grill pan under rack, season and cover with rack. Continue cooking all together for further 20–25 minutes, turning sausages and basting mushrooms and tomatoes. Transfer chops, kidneys and sausages to side of grill pan and place bacon rashers on centre of rack. Return to hot grill and cook bacon on both sides for about 5 minutes. Arrange on hot serving dishes. Garnish with watercress and potato crisps.

Grilled steak

SERVES: ONE

6–8 oz. portion of rump, fillet or sirloin steak
melted butter or oil
salt
freshly ground black pepper

TO GARNISH:

parsley or watercress

Wipe meat and beat the portion with a cutlet bat or rolling pin. Place on grill-pan rack, brush with melted butter or oil and sprinkle with salt and freshly ground black pepper. Place under preheated hot grill and cook for 1 minute on each side to seal juices. Reduce heat and cook for required time (see chart below). Baste with oil during cooking. Garnish with parsley or watercress.

COOKING GUIDE FOR STEAKS

Rare   1-inch thick 7–8 minutes
        $\frac{3}{4}$-inch thick 6–7 minutes.

Medium 1-inch thick 10–13 minutes
        $\frac{3}{4}$-inch thick 9–11 minutes.

Well done 1-inch thick 15–17 minutes
        $\frac{3}{4}$-inch thick 11–13 minutes.

Lamb cutlets with rosemary

SERVES: FOUR

4 trimmed lamb cutlets
2–3 oz. melted butter or margarine
salt and pepper
a little crushed rosemary
4 halved tomatoes
2 lb. creamed potatoes
1 packet (10 oz.) frozen peas

TO GARNISH:

4 cutlet frills
sprigs of parsley

Wipe cutlets with a clean damp cloth. Brush over surface with 1 oz. melted butter or margarine and season with salt, pepper and rosemary. Cover the bone ends of cutlets with aluminium foil. Place halved tomatoes in base of grill pan, dot with remaining fat. Place cutlets on rack of grill pan. Place under medium heat and grill for 3 minutes on each side. Reduce heat to low and continue cooking for 8–10 minutes until tender and cooked through. Meanwhile, prepare creamed potatoes and cook peas according to packet directions. Pipe a border of potato round edge of serving dish and the remainder down the centre of the dish. Stand the cutlets upright in the potato in the centre of dish; remove the foil and replace with paper cutlet frills. Arrange drained peas at either side of the cutlets and tomato halves at the ends. Garnish with parsley.

SPLITTING KIDNEYS

Remove fine outer skin. Cut out core with scissors

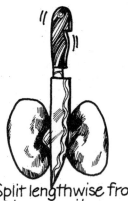

Split lengthwise from side opposite core. Do not cut right through

Open out like a book. Arrange on skewer. Season

Fries and grills

Skewered pork

(*Illustrated left*)

SERVES: TWO

8 oz. pork fillet (or other cut of lean pork)
1 tablespoon cooking oil
salt and pepper
pinch of rosemary
1 can (11½ oz.) sweetcorn kernels

TO GARNISH:
8 oz. firm tomatoes
1 small bunch watercress

Trim the pork and cut into even-sized pieces. Thread on to two long skewers. Brush with oil and sprinkle with salt, pepper and rosemary. Place under a preheated grill and cook, turning as necessary until well cooked through, about 15–20 minutes. Heat the sweetcorn kernels in a small saucepan, drain well then turn into a shallow serving dish. Top with skewered pork and garnish with wedges of raw tomato and a little watercress.

Barbecued gammon rashers

SERVES: FOUR

4 gammon rashers
½ oz. lard

BARBECUE SAUCE:
4 tablespoons vinegar
2 tablespoons redcurrant jelly
2 level teaspoons made mustard
2 tablespoons Demerara sugar
2 level teaspoons paprika pepper

Trim the rind from the gammon rashers. Melt lard in large pan and fry gammon until lightly browned on both sides and cooked through. Keep hot on a plate over a pan of hot water. To serve, coat with the prepared sauce.

TO PREPARE SAUCE: Add vinegar, redcurrant jelly, made mustard, Demerara sugar and the paprika pepper to the pan in which the gammon was cooked. Stir together until heated through and well blended.

Paprika veal

SERVES: FOUR

4 large thin slices of fillet of veal
1 oz. plain flour
4 oz. melted butter
strained juice of 1 lemon
3 medium-sized peeled chopped onions
1 level tablespoon paprika pepper
¼ pint stock (made from chicken stock cube)
¼ pint sour cream

TO GARNISH:
4 lemon wedges
few sprigs of parsley

TO SERVE:
12 oz. freshly boiled rice

Coat veal in the flour, fry in half the melted butter for 3–4 minutes on either side till golden brown and cooked through. Arrange on a hot serving dish, sprinkle with lemon juice, keep hot. Fry peeled and finely chopped onions in remaining 2 oz. melted butter for 10 minutes till tender but not browned. Sprinkle paprika pepper over onions. Blend remaining flour with stock, adding a little at a time to make a smooth paste. Stir in the sour cream. Add to onions, stir well. Heat for few minutes (do not allow to boil). Pour prepared sauce over veal. Garnish with lemon wedges and parsley. Serve with freshly boiled rice.

USEFUL EQUIPMENT

TIMER – invaluable for accuracy. Choose the five hour model

FRENCH COOKS KNIFE – to dice, chop and slice

WOODEN BOWL – and knife with curved blade for chopping

Stews and casseroles

Flemish beef stew

(*Illustrated left*)

SERVES: FOUR

2 lb. lean stewing beef
2 oz. margarine
1 lb. peeled sliced onions
1 pint beer
salt and pepper
a good pinch of thyme
2 bay leaves
2 level tablespoons plain flour
4 tablespoons water
4 lumps sugar
1 tablespoon wine vinegar

Cut the beef into oblong pieces, about 3 inches by 1 inch. Heat the margarine in a frying pan and fry the meat till browned all over. Remove from the frying pan and place in a saucepan. Add peeled and thinly sliced onions to the frying pan and cook for about 10 minutes till lightly brown. Transfer to the saucepan. Mix the beer into the frying pan and stir well to remove any sediment from the pan. Pour the liquid into the saucepan, add the salt, pepper, thyme and bay leaves and bring to the boil. Cover the pan and simmer gently till the meat is tender, about 1½–2½ hours. Blend the flour to a smooth paste with the water and stir into the pan together with the lumps of sugar and wine vinegar. Cook, stirring all the time, till the stew thickens, about 3 minutes.

Lancashire hot-pot

SERVES: FIVE TO SIX

2 lb. potatoes
1 onion
2 oz. mushrooms (optional)
2 lb. middle neck mutton
2 lambs kidneys
2 oz. dripping or cooking fat
1 oz. plain flour
1 pint stock (made from golden stock cube)
salt and pepper
1 teaspoon caster sugar
TO SERVE:
pickled red cabbage

Peel and slice potatoes, onion and mushrooms. Cover base of large casserole with half the sliced potatoes. Trim and cut mutton into even-sized chops. Skin and core kidneys (see p. 43), cut in small pieces. Melt 1 oz. dripping or cooking fat in pan, brown chops all over. Transfer with draining spoon to casserole. Fry kidneys till brown and place on top of mutton. Fry onion in remaining 1 oz. fat until tender. Sprinkle in flour, gradually add stock and stir until sauce thickens. Season well and add caster sugar. Cover kidneys with layer of mushrooms. Pour prepared sauce over. Overlap remaining potato slices on top to cover surface. Cover and cook in moderately slow oven (325 deg. F. —Mark 3) 1¾ hours. Remove cover, return to oven for 15–25 minutes till top browns. Serve with pickled red cabbage.

Oxtail stew

SERVES: THREE TO FOUR

Plan two days in advance.

8 oz. butter beans
1 oxtail
2 onions
2 carrots
1 swede
1 stick celery
2 oz. butter
4 pints water
1 bay leaf
good pinch of marjoram
salt and pepper
2 oz. plain flour
3–4 tablespoons milk

Soak butter beans overnight. Cut the oxtail into pieces. Peel and slice the onions, carrots and swede. Cut the celery into small pieces. Melt butter in saucepan and fry the prepared vegetables 3–4 minutes. Add the oxtail and continue cooking a further 3–4 minutes. Add water, bay leaf and a good pinch of marjoram. Add drained butter beans and seasoning. Bring to the boil then skim the surface. Reduce heat, cover and simmer gently for 3–4 hours. Leave until cold then remove fat from surface. Cook following day for a further 3–4 hours. Blend the flour with milk then stir in a little of the hot liquid from the stew. Gradually stir this mixture into the stew and stir until thickened. Adjust the seasoning if necessary.

SIMPLE BOUQUET GARNI

Place stalks parsley, sprig thyme and a bay leaf, on square of muslin

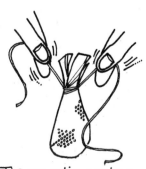

Tie muslin, using thin string, leaving a long end free

Tie string to saucepan handle. Immerse in stew

Stews and casseroles

Pork Oriental

(Illustrated left)
SERVES: FOUR
1½ lb. stewing pork
2–3 tablespoons oil
1 peeled sliced onion
1 oz. plain flour
salt and pepper
½ pint water
1 seeded sliced green pepper
1 can (8 oz.) pineapple pieces
1 tablespoon vinegar
a little soy sauce
1 chicken stock cube
1 can (3½ oz.) pimientos
   (optional)
TO SERVE:
freshly cooked rice

Cut the pork into 1-inch pieces. Heat the oil in a flameproof casserole or pan and fry peeled and sliced onion till lightly brown, then remove from the pan. Toss the prepared meat in the flour, seasoned with salt and pepper, and fry till brown all over. Mix in any remaining flour, water, cooked onion, seeded and sliced green pepper, liquid drained from the pineapple, vinegar, soy sauce and the chicken stock cube. Bring to the boil, stirring, add seasoning to taste and cover. Simmer gently for 1½ hours. Add the pineapple pieces and drained and sliced pimientos, if using, to the pan 15 minutes before the end of cooking time. Serve with rice.

Casserole of liver with mustard dumplings

SERVES: FOUR
1 lb. lambs liver
1 oz. plain flour
salt and pepper
8 oz. onions
4 oz. mushrooms
1 oz. melted lard
6 rashers streaky bacon
¾ pint stock (made from cube)
MUSTARD DUMPLINGS:
4 oz. self-raising flour
pinch of salt
1 level teaspoon dry mustard
2 oz. shredded suet
4 tablespoons milk

Wash liver, dry on kitchen paper. Cut into chunks. Toss in plain flour seasoned with salt and pepper. Peel and slice onions and mushrooms thinly. Fry onions in melted lard until transparent. Trim and chop bacon. Add to pan and cook 2–3 minutes. Add liver and mushrooms. Stir until lightly browned. Sprinkle in remaining flour, gradually blend in stock. Stir until thickened. Turn into casserole. Cover and cook in moderate oven (350 deg. F.—Mark 4) for 25 minutes. Remove cover, season and add dumplings. Cook further 30 minutes.
TO PREPARE DUMPLINGS: Sift self raising flour, salt and dry mustard together into bowl. Stir in suet. Mix to soft dough with milk. Knead lightly on floured board. Divide into eight dumplings.

Osso Buco

SERVES: FOUR
4 pieces hock or knuckle of veal
   (about 2 inches thick)
1 heaped tablespoon plain flour
salt
freshly ground black pepper
3–4 tablespoons olive oil
1 small peeled chopped clove of
   garlic
1 medium-sized peeled chopped
   onion
¼ pint stock or water
¼ pint dry white wine
3 tablespoons tomato purée
TO GARNISH:
chopped parsley
finely grated lemon rind

Dredge the pieces of veal or hock with the flour and season well with the salt and freshly ground black pepper. Heat the olive oil in a pan then put in the meat and cook until browned all over. Add peeled and chopped garlic and onion, stock or water, and dry white wine. Blend in the tomato purée, then cover the pan and leave to simmer gently for about 1½ hours. The meat should be arranged in the pan to remain upright so that the marrow does not fall out of the bone as the meat cooks. Serve sprinkled with chopped parsley and finely grated lemon rind.

BOILING RICE

Cook in boiling salted water about 12 minutes until just tender

Strain in colander Rinse with very hot water to separate grains

Stand colander over steaming water, cover with cloth 2 minutes

Mince

Beefburgers
(*Illustrated left*)

SERVES: SIX

1½ lb. minced raw beef
1¼ teaspoons grated onion
3 oz. fresh white breadcrumbs
1 level teaspoon mixed herbs
½ level teaspoon dry mustard
salt and pepper
a little beaten egg
cooking oil or fat for frying

TO SERVE:

Tomato sauce (see p. 188)

TO GARNISH:

parsley
black and green olives

Mix the beef with grated onion, breadcrumbs, herbs and dry mustard. Season well with salt and pepper. Bind together with a little beaten egg then, with floured hands, form into six cakes about 1 inch thick. Fry in hot fat or oil approximately 8 minutes on each side until well browned and cooked through. Drain well, then place in a prepared Tomato sauce and heat through for 1–2 minutes. Serve on individual plates garnished with parsley and black and green olives.

Country roast

SERVES: FOUR

1 lb. beef sausagemeat
6 oz. raw minced beef
1 onion
2 sticks celery
2 oz. shredded suet
3 oz. fresh white breadcrumbs
¼ level teaspoon salt
good pinch of pepper
2 tablespoons tomato ketchup
good pinch of mixed herbs
2 hard-boiled eggs

TO SERVE:

Tomato sauce (see p. 188)

Mix sausagemeat and minced beef together. Peel onion, chop finely, scrub celery, cut into small pieces. Add to meat together with suet, breadcrumbs, salt, pepper, tomato ketchup and mixed herbs. Bind mixture round 2 hard-boiled eggs. Wrap closely in kitchen foil. Place on baking tin and bake in moderately hot oven (375 deg. F.—Mark 5) for 1¼ hours. Turn back foil, cook 15 minutes. Serve with Tomato sauce.

Moussaka

SERVES: FOUR TO SIX

1½ lb. cooked lamb
1½ lb. peeled potatoes
4 oz. butter
1 large chopped onion
6 tablespoons tomato ketchup
1 tablespoon finely chopped parsley
salt and pepper
4 tablespoons cooking oil
2 sliced aubergines (sprinkled with salt)
4 peeled sliced tomatoes
2 crushed cloves of garlic
Cheese sauce (see p. 186)
3 tablespoons grated Parmesan cheese

Dice or mince cooked lamb. Slice potatoes thinly and dry thoroughly in cloth. Melt 2 oz. butter in heavy pan and fry potatoes until crisp and golden. Use a third of these to line base of ovenproof dish. Fry onion in remaining butter till tender, add lamb and cook 1 minute, stir in tomato ketchup, parsley and seasoning. Spoon into casserole and top with remaining potato slices. Heat oil in a pan and gently cook drained aubergines for 5–6 minutes. Add sliced tomatoes and garlic, cover and cook 3–4 minutes. Arrange on top of potato slices. Pour over prepared sauce, sprinkle with grated Parmesan cheese and place in hot oven (400 deg. F.—Mark 6) about 20 minutes till brown and bubbling.

FRIED ONION RINGS

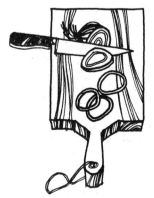

Cut peeled onions into ¼ inch slices, separate into rings

Dip in milk then toss in seasoned flour

Fry rings in hot deep fat, drain well

Mince

Pain de veau roulé (Veal loaf)

(*Illustrated left*)
SERVES: EIGHT
12 oz. shortcrust pastry (see
   p. 192)
beaten egg to glaze
FILLING:
2 oz. butter
1 small peeled chopped onion
4 oz. sausagemeat
1 lb. raw minced veal
1 level teaspoon thyme
1 level tablespoon finely chopped
   parsley
salt and pepper

Place a sheet of greaseproof paper on pastry board. Sprinkle with flour and roll pastry in an oblong 12 by 10 inches and trim. Place filling along centre, damp pastry edges and form into roll using paper to help. Press together to seal along top and ends. Stand join side down on a greased baking tray. Roll trimmings out, cut into $\frac{1}{4}$-inch strips, arrange on roll in criss-cross pattern. Brush with beaten egg. Bake just above centre in a moderately slow oven (325 deg. F.—Mark 3) for 1–1$\frac{1}{2}$ hours or till golden.
TO PREPARE FILLING: Melt butter and fry peeled and chopped onion till tender. Mix in the sausagemeat and cook, stirring, for a few minutes. Mix in minced veal and cook, stirring, for 5 minutes. Add thyme, parsley and seasoning. Cool before using.

Lamb and parsnip pie

SERVES: FOUR
2 lb. parsnips
2 oz. margarine
salt and pepper
1 level teaspoon made mustard
2 tablespoons milk
2 oz. finely grated cheese
8 oz. minced cold cooked lamb
   or mutton
5–6 tablespoons gravy
2 tablespoons fresh white
   breadcrumbs

Wash and peel the parsnips and cook in boiling salted water until tender, about 25 minutes. Drain well, then mash until smooth. Beat in 1 oz. margarine and season well with salt, pepper and mustard. Beat in milk. Spread half the prepared creamed parsnips in the bottom of a greased fireproof dish. Sprinkle with 1 oz. of finely grated cheese. Moisten the cooked lamb or mutton with gravy, then spread over the cheese in the dish. Cover with the remaining creamed parsnips. Sprinkle with the breadcrumbs and remaining cheese and dot with remaining margarine. Bake in moderate oven (350 deg. F.—Mark 4) for 25–30 minutes.

Spaghetti Bolognese

SERVES: FOUR
2 onions
8 oz. carrots
3 sticks celery
1 clove of garlic (optional)
4 tablespoons cooking oil
1 oz. butter
12 oz. minced raw beef
$\frac{1}{2}$ pint dry Italian wine or beef
   stock
4 tablespoons tomato purée
1 bay leaf
1 lb. peeled tomatoes
salt and pepper
12 oz. uncooked spaghetti
a little melted butter
TO SERVE:
finely grated Parmesan cheese

Peel and chop onions and carrots. Wash and slice celery. Finely chop garlic, if using. Heat oil and butter, add prepared vegetables and fry gently for 5 minutes. Mix in minced beef, cook, stirring, till lightly brown. Add the dry Italian wine or stock, tomato purée, bay leaf, peeled tomatoes and seasoning to taste. Bring to boil, cover and cook gently for 30–45 minutes. Remove bay leaf. Cook spaghetti in boiling salted water (see sketches). Drain well, toss in butter. Turn on to large serving dish, top with meat sauce. Serve with Parmesan cheese.

COOKING SPAGHETTI

Hold spaghetti at one end

Gently lower into saucepan of boiling salted water

Cook gently till tender, drain well

Meat pies and puddings

Suet crust pastry

8 oz. self-raising flour
½ level teaspoon salt
4 oz. shredded or finely chopped suet
8 tablespoons water

Sift flour and salt into a bowl. Stir in shredded or chopped suet and mix to a firm but pliable dough with water. Knead on lightly floured board until smooth. Roll out one third of prepared suet crust for lid. Roll out remainder on lightly floured board into large round. Line a 2-pint pudding basin (see sketches below).

The suet crust pastry recipe given on this page is for a steamed pudding. The same pastry can however be used very successfully to cover pies, form into dumplings for stews or make baked savoury or sweet roly-poly.

Steak, kidney and mushroom pudding

(*Illustrated left*)
SERVES: FOUR
FILLING:
1 lb. lean stewing steak
4 oz. ox kidney
4 oz. mushrooms
1 large onion
1 rounded tablespoon plain flour
½ level teaspoon salt
¼ level teaspoon ground pepper
6 tablespoons stock or water
PASTRY:
basic suet crust pastry (see recipe left)

TO PREPARE FILLING: Trim and cut the meat into small neat pieces. Skin, core and roughly chop kidney. Wash mushrooms and cut into quarters. Peel and chop the onion. Toss the meats, mushrooms and onion in flour, salt and pepper. Place into pastry-lined basin then pour in 6 tablespoons stock or water to moisten. Damp edges of pastry. Roll out reserved pastry for lid. Place in position then press edges together to seal firmly. Use a sharp knife to trim the edges neatly. Cover the top closely with aluminium foil. Place in top of a steamer and steam steadily for about 4 hours, refilling bottom pan with boiling water as necessary. Remove foil from pudding. Arrange napkin round bowl for holding and serve immediately.

Steak and kidney pie

SERVES: FOUR
8 oz. packet ready-made puff or home-made shortcrust pastry (see p. 192)
beaten egg
FILLING:
1 lb. stewing steak
8 oz. sheeps kidneys
1 oz. dripping
1 small chopped onion
1 tablespoon plain flour
1 dessertspoon Worcester sauce
1 tablespoon tomato purée
½ pint stock (made from beef stock cube)
salt and pepper

Make pastry if not using the ready-prepared variety.
TO MAKE FILLING: Trim and cut steak into cubes; skin, core and chop kidneys. Melt dripping in pan, add onion, steak and kidneys and toss in hot fat until lightly browned. Stir in flour, mix well, then add Worcester sauce, tomato purée and stock. Season to taste, bring to boil, reduce heat and simmer about 1¾ hours or until tender. Place in 1½-pint pie dish, allow to cool. Damp edges of pie dish and cover with rolled out pastry. Rough up edges and flute. Make pastry leaves with trimmings and damp before putting on pastry. Brush top of pie with beaten egg. Bake in hot oven (400 deg. F.—Mark 6) for 45 minutes or until golden.

LINING A BASIN WITH SUET CRUST

Place basin in centre of rolled out dough to measure sides

Line bowl with pastry, pressing in gently. Put in filling

Roll remaining pastry for lid. Damp edges. Press in place. Trim

Meat pies and puddings

Hot water crust pastry

1 lb. plain flour
¾ level teaspoon salt
6 oz. lard
10 tablespoons water

Sift flour and salt into warm bowl and make a well in centre. Place lard and water into saucepan, bring to boil then at once remove from heat. Pour liquid into centre of flour and mix rapidly with wooden spoon until pastry is cool enough to handle. Knead the dough with hands until the pastry is quite smooth and free from cracks. Shape into a neat round, cut off one third of dough for the lid, then keep this on one side in a warm bowl covered with a cloth. (Pastry must be kept warm enough to mould but not so warm it cannot retain its shape.) Mould remaining pastry inside a greased and floured 6-inch loose-bottomed cake tin (see sketches below). Mark edges with fork, place decoration in position and brush top with beaten egg.

Chunky pork pie
(*Illustrated left*)

SERVES: SIX TO EIGHT
HOT WATER CRUST PASTRY: See recipe above
1 small egg for glazing
FILLING:
1¼ lb. lean pork
1 small onion
¾ level teaspoon salt
¼ level teaspoon pepper
1 level teaspoon powdered sage

JELLIED STOCK:
pork bones
4–5 whole peppercorns
salt
¼ oz. powdered gelatine

Mould pastry inside greased and floured 6-inch tin and make up pie (see sketches below). Keep trimmings for decoration. Make hole in centre of pie. Mark edges with fork. Decorate with pastry leaves. Glaze with beaten egg. Bake in hot oven (400 deg. F.—Mark 6) 30 minutes then reduce heat to moderate (350 deg. F.—Mark 4) and cook for 1 hour. Carefully remove pie from tin, glaze well with remaining beaten egg. Return to oven for 30 minutes. Fill hot pie with jellied stock. Leave in cool place to set.
TO PREPARE FILLING: Cut pork into small cubes. Place in bowl. Peel and chop onion finely. Add to meat with salt, pepper and sage. Mix well.
TO PREPARE JELLIED STOCK: Place bones in saucepan with peppercorns and water to cover. Bring to boil. Reduce heat and simmer gently 1 hour. Strain and add salt to taste. Dissolve gelatine in ¼ pint of the stock and pour into pie through centre hole using funnel or good pouring jug.
To serve hot, omit jellied stock.

Veal, ham and egg pie

SERVES: SIX TO EIGHT
Hot water crust pastry (see recipe left)
FILLING:
1 lb. lean veal (reserve bones for stock)
2 hard-boiled eggs
4 oz. chopped raw ham or bacon
1 dessertspoon chopped parsley
1 level teaspoon lemon thyme
1 level teaspoon salt
½ level teaspoon pepper
JELLIED STOCK:
veal bones
4–5 whole peppercorns
salt
¼ oz. powdered gelatine

Mould pastry inside greased and floured 6-inch cake tin, and make up pie (see sketches below). Keep trimmings for decoration. Make hole in centre of pie, mark edges with fork. Decorate with pastry leaves. Glaze with beaten egg. Bake in hot oven (400 deg. F. —Mark 6) for 30 minutes then reduce heat to moderate (350 deg. F.—Mark 4) and continue cooking 1 hour. Carefully remove pie from tin, glaze well with remaining beaten egg and return to oven for 30 minutes. Fill hot pie with stock. Leave in cool place to set.
TO PREPARE FILLING: Trim veal, cut into small cubes. Coarsely chop hard-boiled eggs. Place eggs, ham or bacon, parsley, thyme and seasoning in bowl. Mix well.
TO PREPARE JELLIED STOCK: See in recipe for Chunky pork pie, left.

RAISING A PIE

Put ⅓ dough aside, cover. Mould rest inside loose-based cake tin

Work pastry up sides of tin. Leave 5 minutes to set. Add filling

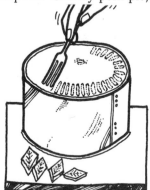
Make decorative leaves, Form lid, damp edges. Press on top. Decorate

Cold meat

Mixed meat salad

(*Illustrated left*)

SERVES: SIX

8 oz. piece salami
8 oz. cooked ham
8 oz. cooked chicken
8 oz. cooked pork
1 can (12½ oz.) asparagus tips
   drained and chopped

DRESSING:

¼ teaspoon salt
¼ teaspoon pepper
¼ teaspoon dry mustard
3 tablespoons oil
1 tablespoon vinegar
1 teaspoon chopped chives
1 teaspoon chopped parsley

MUSTARD MAYONNAISE:

4 tablespoons mayonnaise
1 teaspoon made mustard
3 level teaspoons turmeric
   powder

TO SERVE:

Green salad (see p. 98)

Cut the meats into neat slices or pieces and place in a bowl together with drained and chopped asparagus tips, reserving eight tips for garnish. Place all dressing ingredients in a screw-top jar and shake till well blended. Pour over the meats and mix well. Allow to stand for 30 minutes. Turn into a serving dish and arrange the drained asparagus tips on top. Serve with Mustard mayonnaise and Green salad.

TO PREPARE MUSTARD MAYONNAISE: Combine the mayonnaise, mustard and turmeric powder well together.

Norfolk brawn

SERVES: EIGHT

Plan two days in advance

half hock of salted pork
   (approximately 4½ lb.)
pinch of powdered sage
salt
pepper

TO SERVE:

Green salad (see p. 98)

Soak the pork in cold water for 12 hours. Lift pork into a saucepan and cover with fresh cold water. Bring to the boil, strain off water, cover with fresh cold water, bring back to the boil, cover and simmer till the meat starts to come away from the bone, about 4–5 hours. Lift the pork from the pan, remove all the meat from the bone. Put the bone back in the pan and simmer till about ½ pint stock is left in the pan. Cut meat into very fine pieces and mix in powdered sage and seasoning to taste. Add the ½ pint strained stock, mix well. Turn into wetted 2½-pint basin or mould. Allow to set in a cool place. Turn out when firm. Serve with Green salad.

Pressed ox tongue

SERVES: SIX TO EIGHT

Plan two or three days in advance

1 medium-sized salted ox tongue
1 small peeled onion
1 carrot
2 bay leaves
a few peppercorns
¼ oz. gelatine
3 tablespoons hot water

Order the salted ox tongue a few days in advance. Wash thoroughly, soak in cold water overnight. Place the tongue in fresh water to cover in a large saucepan. Bring to the boil, boil for 5 minutes then drain off the liquid. Add more fresh water to cover the tongue and add peeled onion, carrot, bay leaves and peppercorns. Bring to the boil, then reduce heat and simmer very gently for 3–4 hours or till tongue is really tender. Allow the tongue to cool slightly in the liquor then lift out and drain. Carefully strip off skin and trim the root and remove bones. Arrange in a 6-inch cake tin (see sketches below). Dissolve gelatine in hot water, blend with ¼ pint of the stock from cooked tongue. Pour into the cake tin over the tongue then cover with a plate that will fit inside the tin and place a heavy weight on top. Put in cold place to set overnight. Turn out, cut in slices.

PRESSING TONGUE

Curl cooked tongue round in cake tin. It should fit closely

Strain stock over

Place plate on tongue and top with heavy weight

Cold meat

Stuffed ham rolls
(*Illustrated left*)
SERVES: SIX
6 slices cooked ham
3 tablespoons home-made
  mayonnaise (see p. 189)
3 tablespoons single cream
4 oz. Cheddar cheese
2-inch piece chopped cucumber
3 finely shredded lettuce leaves
salt and pepper
½ pint prepared aspic (made from
  crystals)
TO GARNISH:
1 tomato
8 black olives
few lettuce leaves

Trim ham if necessary, put aside. Mix the mayonnaise with the cream, grated Cheddar cheese, chopped cucumber and finely shredded lettuce leaves. Season to taste. Place spoonfuls of the mixture on to ham, roll up. Cover a serving dish with a thin layer of aspic and allow to set. Place the ham rolls neatly on dish and coat with aspic, leave until set. Pour remaining aspic into a wetted shallow tin and place in refrigerator until firm. Turn aspic out of tin on to wetted greaseproof paper, cut into cubes with wet round-bladed knife. Arrange wedges of tomato across ham rolls and garnish edge of dish with cubes of aspic, black olives and lettuce leaves.

Doria sausages
SERVES: FOUR
1 lb. pork or beef chipolata
  sausages
½ oz. cooking fat
1 small peeled sliced cucumber
1 can (4 oz.) pimientos, drained
  and sliced
6 chopped gherkins
12 oz. cooked cold diced new
  potatoes
2–3 tablespoons mayonnaise
salt and pepper
1 lettuce

Fry chipolata sausages in melted fat until golden brown, about 20 minutes. Leave to cool. Mix the peeled and diced cucumber with drained sliced pimientos, chopped gherkins and diced potatoes, then bind with the mayonnaise and season to taste. Wash the lettuce and arrange on serving dish. Pile the salad mixture in centre and arrange sausages round the edge.

Glazed meat loaf
SERVES: SIX
1 onion
1 oz. cooking fat
1½ lb. raw minced beef
4 oz. fresh white breadcrumbs
4 tablespoons stock or water
2 teaspoons tomato purée
1 beaten egg
pinch of mixed dried herbs
salt and pepper
TO GARNISH:
1 firm tomato
small sprigs of parsley
1 basket cress
GLAZE:
1 teaspoon meat or vegetable
  extract
4–5 tablespoons water
½ level teaspoon powdered
  gelatine

Peel and chop the onion then fry in melted fat until brown. Stir in minced beef and cook, stirring until brown all over. Remove from heat and stir in the fresh breadcrumbs, stock or water, tomato purée, beaten egg, mixed dried herbs and seasoning. Mix well and turn into greased 2-lb. loaf tin. Bake in a moderately hot oven (375 deg. F.—Mark 5) for 1 hour. Turn out. When really cold, coat with prepared glaze, and garnish (see sketches below). When set, transfer to dish.
TO PREPARE GLAZE: Place meat or vegetable extract, water and powdered gelatine in a pan and heat until gelatine has dissolved. Use when just beginning to set.

GLAZING MEAT LOAF

Turn cooked meat loaf on to wire rack. Cool

Leave glaze till just beginning to set. Spoon over top

Garnish top with pieces of tomato and parsley

Chef's special

Steak au poivre (Pepper steak)
(*Illustrated left*)

SERVES: FOUR

4 rump or porterhouse steaks (about ¾ inch thick)
1 tablespoon whole black peppercorns
1 oz. butter
1 tablespoon oil
1 tablespoon Cognac
¼ pint double cream

TO GARNISH:
tomato wedges

TO SERVE:
Green salad (see p. 98)
sauté or boiled potatoes

Trim the steaks. Crush the black peppercorns in a pestle and mortar, or place in a cloth and crush with a rolling pin. Coat the steaks well with crushed peppercorns, pressing them into the meat. Leave for 1 hour. Place the butter and oil in a frying pan, and when hot fry the steaks quickly about 2–3 minutes on each side for rare steaks, 5–6 minutes on each side for medium to well cooked. Place steaks on serving dish. Add Cognac then stir cream into pan and bring almost to boil then pour over the steak. Garnish with tomato wedges. Serve with green salad and sauté or boiled potatoes.

VARIATIONS

Instead of serving with the cream sauce as in the recipe left the steak can be coated well in the crushed peppercorns, left for 1 hour and then fried 2–3 minutes on each side and served with the juices from the pan. This dish is quickly made but should be served immediately. If liked the steak can be cooked as above and served with the following sauce which can be prepared in advance. Peel and chop 1 clove of garlic and sauté in 2 tablespoons oil until transparent. Add 1 medium can (14 oz.) peeled tomatoes and salt and pepper to taste. Cook quickly 15 minutes. Stir in 1 tablespoon finely chopped parsley and ½ level teaspoon oregano or marjoram. Pour over the prepared steaks and serve.

Salade Niçoise
page 99

□

Steak au poivre
Spinach
Creamed potatoes

□

Lemon sorbet
page 119

Suggested wines for main course:
Côtes du Rhône

or

Gigondas

STEAK AU POIVRE

Lightly crush black peppercorns between folds of tea towel

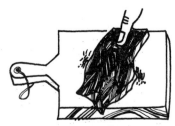

Press onto each side of steak

Leave for at least one hour before cooking

Chef's special

Crown roast of lamb
(*Illustrated left*)

SERVES: SIX

1 crown roast

STUFFING:

1 small onion
1 oz. melted butter
minced trimmings from joint
3 oz. fresh white breadcrumbs
1 level teaspoon mixed herbs
salt and pepper
1 small beaten egg

TO GARNISH:

2 tablespoons freshly boiled
 buttered new potatoes
2 heaped tablespoons each freshly
 cooked peas and freshly
 cooked peeled diced carrots
washed watercress
cutlet frills

Ask your butcher to prepare the crown roast joint. It is made from 2 best ends of neck of lamb, containing 14 cutlets, still joined at their base after the chine has been removed. Ask your butcher to mince the meat trimmings as you can include them in the stuffing.

Place crown roast in meat tin. Fill centre with prepared stuffing. Cover ends of bones and stuffing with aluminium foil. Roast on centre shelf of a moderate oven (350 deg. F.—Mark 4) for 1½ hours. Remove cover from stuffing and return joint to oven for further 10–15 minutes to brown. Remove foil from cutlet ends and cover with cutlet frills. Transfer joint to a serving dish. Arrange prepared garnish of buttered new potatoes, cooked peas and peeled diced carrots in neat groups at either end of the dish. Place sprigs of watercress down sides of dish.

TO PREPARE STUFFING: Peel and finely chop onion. Cook in melted butter for 2–3 minutes till tender. Add minced trimmings and cook for a further minute. Remove from heat, add breadcrumbs, mixed herbs and seasoning. Bind together with beaten egg.

VARIATIONS

If preferred the crown roast may be cooked without any stuffing and served with the centre filled with diced mixed vegetables, creamed potatoes, buttered peas. Alternatively a well-seasoned sausagemeat packed into the centre cavity before roasting can be very tasty.

For a Lamb Guard of Honour (*Illustrated on the jacket*), order 2 best ends of neck of lamb, each with the same number of cutlets. Remove the chine bone from each joint and trim and clean the bone tips. Place the two joints in a meat tin, pressing the bones together to cross in the centre and protrude at each side. Cover the bone tips and roast as for crown roast. To serve, place on a dish and cover each bone tip with a cutlet frill. Surround with a selection of vegetables.

Cream of mushroom soup
page 14

□

Crown roast of lamb
Buttered peas
Carrots
Buttered new potatoes

□

Rich continental cheesecake
page 115

Suggested wine for main course:
Barolo

SHAPING
CUTLET FRILLS

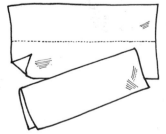

Cut strips of paper
2 inches by 5 inches
Fold in half lengthwise

Cut at intervals
of ⅛ inch along
double edge

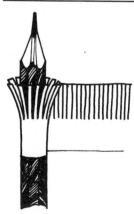

Wind strip round pencil
about three times,
secure with glue

Chef's special

Paupiettes de veau
(*Illustrated left*)

SERVES: SIX

6 even-sized escalopes of veal
6 rashers back bacon
1–2 small onions
4 oz. mushrooms
2 oz. butter
1 bay leaf
2–3 oz. fresh white breadcrumbs
good pinch of thyme
salt and pepper
2 oz. butter for frying

TO GARNISH:
parsley
fluffy mashed potatoes

Ask your butcher to beat the escalopes of veal. Trim rind from bacon rashers and discard, then cut away the fat from each rasher in one piece and reserve. Chop bacon. Peel, slice and finely chop onions and mushrooms and add to chopped bacon. Fry in butter in frying pan with bay leaf until onion is tender. Remove bay leaf, add breadcrumbs, thyme, salt and pepper and cook a further minute. Divide mixture evenly between 6 escalopes of veal and fold each one up like a parcel, so that the filling is completely enclosed. Wrap reserved strips of bacon fat round each escalope and secure with strong cotton or fine string. Heat butter in frying pan and fry the paupiettes until brown all over, turning frequently, then reduce heat and cover with lid and cook for further 20–25 minutes or until tender and cooked through. Remove cotton or string. Serve garnished with parsley and fluffy mashed potatoes.

VARIATIONS

If liked a sauce may be made to serve with the above recipe in the following way: add a wineglass dry white wine to the pan after the cooked paupiettes have been transferred to a hot serving dish. Stir well to remove any sediment from sides of pan then cook rapidly 2–3 minutes. Season to taste.

Instead of spreading a prepared stuffing over the meat a very tasty dish can be made by placing a thin slice of Gruyère cheese on top of each fillet before folding it over and tying it up as shown.

Watercress cream soup
page 15

□

Paupiettes de veau
Cauliflower
with white sauce
Buttered new potatoes

□

Summer fruit salad
page 111

Suggested wine for main course:
Château La Tour Alain

STUFFING PAUPIETTES of VEAL

Divide prepared stuffing between trimmed escalopes

Fold over ends. Roll up neatly to enclose stuffing

Place fat bacon over join, then tie with fine string

Meat menus

Melon with prawn cocktail
page 8

□

Grilled steak
page 43

Gina's salad
page 99

Potato crisps

□

Summer fruit salad
page 111

Gazpacho
page 17

□

Skewered pork
page 45

Boiled rice

Simple salad
page 98

□

Cherries in wine
page 111

Tomatoes Monaco
page 11

□

Paprika veal
page 45

Spinach—Italian style
page 91

Creamed potatoes

□

Fiesta pancakes
page 106

Salade Niçoise
page 99

□

Flemish beef stew
page 47

Boiled potatoes

Red cabbage
page 93

□

Apricot walnut sponge
page 106

Custard

Grilled grapefruit
page 9

□

Roast lamb continental style
page 40

Baked beetroot in white sauce
page 95

Creamed potatoes

□

Brandied fruit pie
page 107

Cream

Hors-d'œuvre eggs
page 11

□

Pork Oriental
page 49

Boiled potatoes

Green salad
page 98

□

Lemon sorbet
page 119

Mixed hors-d'œuvre
page 11

□

Lamb cutlets with rosemary
page 43

Chicory in cheese sauce
page 93

Jacket baked potatoes
page 157—sketch

□

Sunset apples
page 113

Stuffed eggs
page 8

□

Baked forehock with pineapple and sweetcorn
page 41

Potato croquettes
page 90

□

Treacle tart
page 107

Salmon cream in lemon cups
page 8

□

Mixed grill
page 43

Watercress

Potato crisps

□

**Melon with
rich vanilla ice cream**
page 117

Minestrone
page 15

□

Barbecued gammon rashers
page 45

Parsnip chips
page 95

Creamed potatoes

□

**Chocolate pudding
with fudge sauce**
page 109

Vichyssoise
page 17

□

Moussaka
page 51

Coleslaw
page 101

□

Hot apricot slices
page 113

Normandy salad
page 11

□

Savoury roast pork
page 40

Jacket baked potatoes
page 157—sketch

Red cabbage
page 93

□

Caramel custard
page 115

Tomato soup
page 14

□

**Roast sirloin of beef
with Yorkshire pudding**
page 40

Roast potatoes

Buttered sprouts

□

Tarte à l'orange
page 121

Melon
page 8

□

**Liver casserole
with mustard dumplings**
page 49

Jacket baked potatoes
page 157—sketch

Carrots

□

Country house pear pie
page 107

Cream

Watercress cream soup
page 15

□

Chunky pork pie
page 57

New potatoes

Buttered peas

□

Lemon soufflé pie
page 115

**Tomatoes in
sweet and sour dressing**
page 11

□

Steak and kidney pie
page 55

Vegetable croquettes
page 90

Watercress

□

Bananas in foil
page 113

Poultry and Game

Chicken
Duckling
Turkey
Rabbit and game
Chef's specials
Menus

Roast chicken with celery stuffing (*recipe overleaf*)

Chicken

Roast chicken with celery stuffing

SERVES: FOUR

1 dressed chicken (about 3 lb.)
2 oz. butter
Celery stuffing (see p. 191)

SAVOURY RICE:

2 oz. butter
6 oz. long grain rice
¾ pint chicken stock made from giblets
1 bay leaf
salt and pepper
2 oz. stoned black olives

TO GARNISH:

1 oz. salted peanuts
celery leaves or watercress

Stuff chicken, weigh and calculate cooking time allowing 20 minutes to the lb. and 20 minutes over. Stand chicken in roasting tin and spread with butter. Cover with kitchen foil. Place in moderately hot oven (375 deg. F.—Mark 5) for calculated cooking time. Open foil 15 minutes before end to allow for browning. Place chicken on serving dish with prepared rice. Sprinkle with salted peanuts and garnish with celery leaves or watercress.

TO PREPARE SAVOURY RICE: Heat 1 oz. of the butter in pan, add rice and cook gently 1–2 minutes till the rice has absorbed the fat. Add stock, bay leaf, salt and pepper. Bring to the boil. Cover and simmer 15–20 minutes till rice is tender and the liquid absorbed. Stir in black olives and remaining butter.

New England chicken casserole

SERVES: FOUR

1 dressed chicken (approximately 3 lb.)
2 oz. plain flour seasoned with salt and pepper
6 small firm tomatoes
2 oz. butter
1 medium-sized peeled chopped onion
1 can (8 oz.) tomato juice
¾ pint stock (made from chicken stock cube)
1 bay leaf
¼ level teaspoon nutmeg
1 can (8 oz.) sweetcorn kernels

TO SERVE:

boiled rice

With a strong sharp knife split the chicken in half through the breastbone and then the backbone. Cut each half into two joints, i.e. wing and leg portions. Toss the joints in seasoned flour, reserving remaining flour for sauce. Blanch and peel tomatoes (see p. 11). Melt butter in pan and fry joints until golden brown. Transfer to a casserole. Fry peeled chopped onion in remaining fat till tender. Stir in remaining flour, cook for 1 minute. Add tomato juice, blend in stock, stirring till sauce thickens. Pour the sauce over chicken. Add bay leaf and nutmeg. Cover and cook in moderate oven (350 deg. F.—Mark 4) for 1 hour. Remove bay leaf, add drained sweetcorn kernels and tomatoes. Return to oven for 30 minutes. Serve with rice.

Chicken with cucumber sauce

SERVES: FOUR TO SIX

1 boiling chicken (4 lb. dressed weight)
2–3 pints water
1 chicken stock cube
a few strips lemon rind
1 bay leaf
salt and pepper
1 small onion
1 cucumber
2 oz. butter
1 oz. plain flour
2 tablespoons cream
good squeeze of lemon juice

TO GARNISH:

1 tablespoon chopped parsley

Wipe chicken and place in large pan with water, add chicken stock cube, lemon rind, bay leaf, salt and pepper. Bring to boil, cover and simmer 2–2½ hours or until tender. Peel, slice and chop onion. Cut cucumber into dice. Remove chicken from pan, cool slightly, strip away skin; strain ½ pint stock from pan for sauce. Return chicken to remaining stock in pan, keep hot. Melt 1 oz. butter in another pan, add onion and cucumber, cook gently 1 minute. Stir in flour, gradually blend in stock, simmer gently, for 10–15 minutes. Cool slightly, then add remaining butter, cream and lemon juice. Transfer chicken to serving dish and coat with sauce. Sprinkle with chopped parsley.

TRUSSING CHICKEN

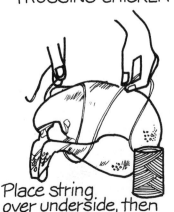

Place string over underside, then round legs

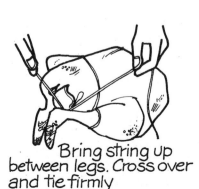

Bring string up between legs. Cross over and tie firmly

Take strings alongside chicken, lock under wings, tie firmly

Forester's casserole

SERVES: FOUR TO FIVE

4–5 chicken joints
2–3 oz. butter
1 large onion
8 oz. small peeled button mushrooms
2 level tablespoons plain flour
1 bottle (10 oz.) pure apple juice
¼ pint stock
salt
freshly ground black pepper
2–3 tablespoons cream or top of
  the milk
TO GARNISH:
chopped parsley

Fry chicken joints in hot butter, turning until golden brown all over. Transfer to casserole or ovenproof dish. Peel and chop onion and fry in remaining butter in pan until just transparent. Add peeled button mushrooms, cook until tender. Sprinkle in flour. Gradually blend in apple juice and stock, then stir over gentle heat until sauce thickens. Season well with salt and black pepper. Pour prepared sauce over chicken joints in casserole, cover with lid or kitchen foil. Cook in moderate oven (350 deg. F.—Mark 4) for about 1 hour. Stir in cream or top of the milk just before serving. Sprinkle with chopped parsley.

Lemon chicken pie

SERVES: FOUR TO SIX

FILLING:
1 boiling chicken (3½–4 lb.
  dressed weight)
3–4 pints water
1 peeled onion
1 bay leaf
6 peppercorns
salt
SAUCE:
½ pint white sauce (see p. 186)
  made with ¼ pint chicken stock
  and ¼ pint milk
finely grated rind and juice of 1
  lemon
salt and pepper
1 packet (5 oz.) frozen peas,
  cooked and drained
PASTRY:
8 oz. puff pastry
beaten egg

Place the chicken, whole, and giblets in pan with water, peeled onion, bay leaf, peppercorns and salt. Bring to the boil, cover and simmer gently 3 hours. Remove from pan, cut into portions. Add finely grated rind and juice of lemon, seasoning and cooked drained peas into prepared sauce. Arrange chicken and sauce in layers in 1½-pint dish. Roll out pastry and cover dish (see step-by-step on p. 192). Glaze with beaten egg. Bake just above centre of very hot oven (450 deg. F.—Mark 8) 10–15 minutes. Reduce heat to hot (400 deg. F.—Mark 6) for further 20–25 minutes until cooked.

Chicken pâté

SERVES: SIX TO EIGHT

1 lb. cold cooked chicken
8 oz. cooked ham
3 oz. fresh white breadcrumbs
8 chopped pickled walnuts
2 chicken stock cubes
1 oz. powdered gelatine
1 pint boiling water
salt and pepper
½ teaspoon Worcester sauce
TO GARNISH:
2 sliced hard-boiled eggs
watercress

Finely mince the chicken and ham. Mix the minced meats with the fresh white breadcrumbs and the chopped pickled walnuts. Dissolve the chicken stock cubes and the powdered gelatine in the boiling water. Allow to cool and then add the chicken and ham mixture. Mix very thoroughly and add salt, pepper and Worcester sauce to taste. Turn the mixture into a 2-pint pudding basin and press down well. Place a piece of kitchen foil over the top of the basin and leave in a cool place to set. Turn on to serving dish and garnish with sliced eggs and watercress.

CARVING CHICKEN

Remove one leg with sharp knife

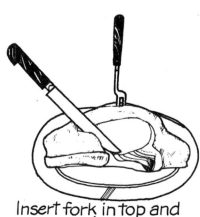

Insert fork in top and remove wing

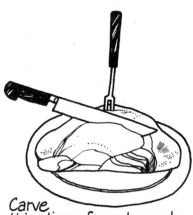

Carve thin slices from breast. Repeat procedure other side

Chicken

Chicken casserole with lemon

(*Illustrated left*)
SERVES: SIX
6 chicken joints
salt and pepper
2 oz. butter
1 tablespoon oil
1 peeled sliced onion
2 rounded tablespoons plain flour
$\frac{1}{2}$ pint stock (made from chicken
   stock cube)
1 sliced lemon
2 bay leaves
1 level teaspoon sugar

Wipe the chicken joints and sprinkle with salt and pepper. Heat butter and oil in frying pan and fry joints quickly till golden brown all over. Transfer to casserole. Add peeled and sliced onion to frying pan and cook till tender, about 5 minutes. Sprinkle in the flour and cook 1 minute. Blend in the stock and bring to the boil stirring. Add sliced lemon, bay leaves, seasoning and sugar. Pour over chicken. Cover and place in a moderately hot oven (375 deg. F. —Mark 5) for about 45 minutes till chicken is cooked. Remove lid 15 minutes before end of cooking time to allow to brown.

Chicken Andalusia

SERVES: FOUR
1 cold cooked chicken (4 lb.
   dressed weight)
12 oz. long grain rice
pinch of saffron powder
$\frac{1}{2}$ pint home-made mayonnaise
   (see p. 189)
1 can (7 oz.) pimientos
4–6 chopped cocktail gherkins
salt and pepper
a few lettuce leaves
1 oz. toasted split almonds
7 black olives
7 green olives

Cut cold chicken from the bones. Chop dark meat into small pieces and flake white meat into larger pieces. Cook rice in boiling salted water with saffron powder for about 12 minutes or until just tender. Strain through a colander and pour boiling water over to separate grains. Rinse well with cold water and leave to stand in a colander until well drained and completely cold. Add chopped chicken to prepared mayonnaise. Drain pimientos and cut into strips. Add half to the chicken mixture with the chopped gherkins and seasoning to taste. Reserve remaining strips for garnish. Wash and drain lettuce.

TO ASSEMBLE SALAD: Make a border of rice round serving plate. Fill centre with lettuce. Top with chicken mixture. Sprinkle with almonds and decorate with pimientos and black and green olives.

Barbecued chicken

SERVES: TWO
2 chicken halves
3 oz. butter
4 tablespoons malt vinegar
1 tablespoon Worcester sauce
1 tablespoon tomato purée
1 level tablespoon brown sugar
1 teaspoon finely grated or
   chopped onion
1 level teaspoon paprika pepper
$\frac{1}{2}$ teaspoon salt

Skewer each chicken half as flat as possible. Melt the butter in a small saucepan and brush it liberally all over chicken pieces. Arrange chicken halves skin side down in bottom of grill pan and grill gently for 12–15 minutes. Meanwhile, add remaining ingredients to butter left in saucepan and simmer together for 2 minutes. Turn the chicken, brush over with prepared sauce and continue grilling for a further 15–20 minutes or until cooked right through. Serve with remaining hot sauce poured over top.

JOINTING CHICKEN

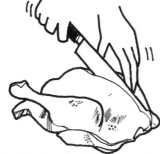

Split in half through breastbone with sharp knife

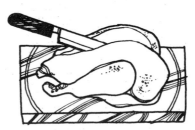

Open chicken out, then cut through length of backbone

Cut each half into wing and leg portions

Duckling

Roast duckling with orange sauce
(*Illustrated left*)

SERVES: FOUR

1 dressed duckling (about 4 lb.), carves into: two portions leg and breast, two portions leg and wing
salt and pepper
1 small peeled onion
1 small peeled apple

TO GARNISH:
1 large orange
a little chopped parsley
potato crisps

ORANGE SAUCE:
juices from the cooked duckling
finely grated rind of 1 orange
juice of 1 orange and $\frac{1}{2}$ lemon made up to $\frac{3}{4}$ pint with stock (made from duck giblets)
2 tablespoons dark brown sugar
salt and pepper
2 tablespoons brandy

Sprinkle duckling with salt and pepper. Cut peeled onion and apple in wedges, place inside bird. Place in roasting tin. Prick skin with a fork. Cook above centre in moderate oven (350 deg. F.—Mark 4) allowing 20 minutes to the lb. plus 20 minutes. Peel and slice orange, dip edges in parsley. Garnish duckling with orange slices and crisps. Serve with orange sauce.

TO PREPARE ORANGE SAUCE: Skim off fat, pour juices from roasting tin into a pan. Add orange rind, stock and dark brown sugar. Boil rapidly 5 minutes. Season. Add brandy before serving.

Roast duckling with cherry sauce

SERVES: FOUR

1 dressed duckling (approximately 4 lb.)
salt and pepper
1 small peeled onion

TO GARNISH:
potato crisps
watercress

CHERRY SAUCE:
juices from the cooked duckling
1 can (16 oz.) stoned black cherries
juice and finely grated rind of 1 lemon
salt and pepper
3 tablespoons brandy (optional)

Wipe the duckling with a clean damp cloth. Sprinkle inside and outside with salt and pepper. Cut the peeled onion into wedges and place inside the bird. Stand the duckling in a roasting tin and prick in several places with a fork. Cook in a moderate oven (350 deg. F. Mark 4) allowing 20 minutes to the lb. and 20 minutes over. Transfer to a serving dish and garnish with potato crisps and watercress. Serve cherry sauce separately.

TO PREPARE CHERRY SAUCE: Skim the fat from the juices in the roasting tin, then pour the juices into a saucepan. Add the drained juice from the cherries, lemon juice and rind, and salt and pepper to taste. Boil rapidly for 5 minutes. Add the cherries and heat well. If liked, add the brandy just before serving.

Casserole of duckling

SERVES: FOUR

1 duckling cut into four portions
salt
freshly ground black pepper
2 onions
1 bay leaf
$\frac{1}{2}$ pint red wine
4 oz. bacon
a little cooking oil
$\frac{3}{4}$ pint stock (made from giblets)
1 carrot
2 sticks celery
4 oz. button mushrooms
grated orange rind

Wipe duckling with a damp cloth, sprinkle with salt and freshly ground black pepper. Peel, slice and chop onions, and place in bowl with seasoned duckling and bay leaf. Pour over red wine and leave to stand in cool place for 2 hours. Remove duck portions with draining spoon, dry on absorbent paper. Reserve liquid. Trim bacon, cut into pieces and cook gently in oil for 3–4 minutes. Add duckling, brown all over in hot oil. Drain well, then place in ovenproof casserole. Cook in moderate oven (350 deg. F.—Mark 4) 15 minutes. Remove from oven, pour over wine mixture and stock. Peel and chop carrot, chop celery, rinse mushrooms and add to casserole. Cover and return to slow oven (300 deg. F.—Mark 2) for further $1\frac{1}{2}$–2 hours or until tender. Skim off excess fat. Sprinkle with rind.

CARVING DUCKLING

Cut off legs with sharp knife. Divide each in two

Cut off wings

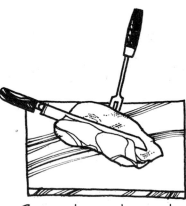
Carve breast meat in long wedge-like slices

Turkey

Roast turkey

(*Illustrated left*)

SERVES: TEN TO SIXTEEN
10–12 lb. dressed turkey
stuffing (see pp. 190–191)
4 oz. soft butter
1 lb. pork sausagemeat
TO GARNISH:
watercress
ACCOMPANIMENTS:
Bread sauce (see p. 188)
Gravy, made with giblet stock (see sketches p. 40)
cranberry sauce or jelly
bacon rolls

Wipe the turkey inside and out with a clean damp cloth. Fill neck end with stuffing, wrap flap of skin over and secure with a skewer. Retruss the bird if necessary. Weigh stuffed bird to calculate cooking time, allowing 25 minutes to the lb. Place turkey on foil in meat tin and spread with soft butter. Cover with aluminium foil (see sketches below). Place in a moderately slow oven (325 deg. F. —Mark 3) for estimated time—30 minutes before end of cooking time turn oven up to hot (425 deg. F.—Mark 7), turn back foil, form sausagemeat into small balls and place round the bird. Place turkey on a hot serving dish with the sausage balls. Garnish with watercress. Serve with accompaniments.

TURKEY COOKING TIMES: Weigh bird after stuffing it and calculate cooking time as follows:

25 minutes to the lb. for a 7 lb.– 12 lb. bird.
20 minutes to the lb. for a 13 lb.– 16 lb. bird.
18 minutes to the lb. for a 17 lb.– 25 lb. bird.

TO PREPARE TURKEY FOR COLD BUFFET:·
Cover bird with strips of streaky bacon or spread with soft butter then wrap in aluminium foil. Stand in a meat tin. Place in a moderately slow oven (325 deg. F.—Mark 3) for all but 30 minutes of the calculated cooking time, then fold the foil back and increase the oven to hot (425 deg. F.—Mark 7) and allow the bird to brown for remaining 30 minutes. Allow to cool.

7 lb. turkey serves six to eight.
10 lb. turkey serves ten to twelve.
12 lb. turkey serves twelve to sixteen.
16 lb. turkey serves sixteen to twenty.
20 lb. turkey serves twenty-five to thirty.

Nutty corn pilaff

SERVES: FOUR
1 medium-sized onion
2 oz. butter
6 oz. long grain rice
1 pint stock (made from chicken stock cube)
1 can (12 oz.) whole sweetcorn kernels, drained
8 oz. diced cold cooked turkey, chicken or pork
2 oz. shredded blanched almonds (lightly toasted)
salt and pepper
TO GARNISH:
2 hard-boiled eggs
2 oz. black olives
little chopped parsley
TO SERVE:
Green salad (see p. 98)
French bread

Peel and chop onion. Fry in 1 oz. melted butter till tender but not browned. Stir in rice and stock. Bring to the boil, cover and simmer for 25 minutes till rice is tender but not broken up and liquid has evaporated. Stir in drained sweetcorn kernels, diced chicken or other cooked meat, almonds and remaining butter, heat through for 10 minutes and season to taste. Turn pilaff into individual serving dishes. Place halved slices of hard-boiled eggs and black olives round border, sprinkle centre with parsley. Serve with a Green salad and French bread.

FOIL ROAST TURKEY

Place turkey on large sheet of foil in roasting tin

Fold foil over to meet in centre. Fold ends in loose parcel

Press edges lightly together to prevent opening

Rabbit and game

Hunter's casserole
(*Illustrated left*)
SERVES: FOUR
1½–2 lb. rabbit joints
6 rashers streaky bacon
3 onions
½ teaspoon mixed herbs
salt and pepper
1 pint stock (made from golden
   stock cube)
1 coarsely grated carrot
TO SERVE:
Jacket baked potatoes (see sketches
   p. 157)

Trim rabbit joints. Remove the bacon rind. Peel and slice onions. Fill casserole with layers of rabbit, bacon, onions, sprinkling mixed herbs and seasoning between each layer. Pour stock over. Cover and cook in moderately slow oven (325 deg. F.—Mark 3) for 1½ hours. Stir in carrot and return to oven for further 30 minutes. Serve with jacket baked potatoes.

Highland grouse
SERVES: TWO
2 young grouse
2 oz. butter
salt and pepper
1 packet (8 oz.) frozen raspberries
grated lemon rind
TO SERVE:
creamed potatoes
green vegetables

Wipe the grouse. Place 1 oz. of butter inside each and sprinkle well with salt and pepper. Lightly mix defrosted raspberries and lemon rind together and spoon most of mixture evenly into the cavity of each bird. Place remainder of mixture round birds. Cover and cook in a hot oven (400 deg. F.—Mark 6) for 35–45 minutes. Remove cover and cook for further 10 minutes. Serve with freshly creamed potatoes and green vegetables.

Roast pheasant with mushrooms
SERVES: TWO
1 dressed pheasant
4 oz. button mushrooms
1 oz. butter
½ level teaspoon salt
pinch cayenne pepper
few rashers fat bacon
FRIED BREADCRUMBS:
1½–2 oz. butter
3 oz. fresh white breadcrumbs

Wipe pheasant with a damp cloth. Wash and dry mushrooms. Cream butter till soft, add salt and cayenne pepper. Mix in the mushrooms. Place this mixture inside the pheasant. Place pheasant in a meat tin and cover with bacon rashers. Cover with a buttered piece of greaseproof paper. Roast on shelf above centre of a hot oven (400 deg. F.—Mark 6) for 30 minutes. Baste pheasant occasionally during cooking. Remove the paper and continue roasting for 10 minutes. Serve with juices from pan and breadcrumbs fried in butter until golden and crisp.

GAME SEASONS

Rabbit: September to February. Imported all the year round

Grouse: August 12th to December 10th. Best mid August to mid October

Pheasant: October 1st to February 1st. Best November to January

Chef's special

Coq au vin
(Illustrated left)

SERVES: FOUR

3–4 lb. chicken
4 oz. piece of fat bacon
  (preferably unsmoked)
20 shallots or small onions
1 clove of garlic
3 oz. butter
1 tablespoon cooking oil
3–4 tablespoons Cognac
1 pint red Burgundy
6 oz. button mushrooms
1 oz. butter

BOUQUET GARNI:

pinch of mixed herbs
1 clove
4 peppercorns
1 bay leaf
1 blade of mace
a few parsley stalks

TO GARNISH:

little chopped parsley

Wipe the chicken, then with a strong knife split it in half through the breastbone and then through the backbone. Cut each half into two joints i.e. the wing and the leg portions. Cut the bacon into 1-inch cubes. Peel the shallots or onions. Peel and crush the clove of garlic in a pestle and mortar or finely chop it. Fry bacon, shallots or onions and garlic in half the butter and the cooking oil in a large frying pan for 10 minutes till lightly browned. Transfer to a plate and keep hot. Add the remaining butter to the pan and fry the chicken joints over a fairly high heat for 10–15 minutes till

browned on all sides. Turn off the heat. Pour the Cognac over the chicken joints, then set it alight. When the flames have died down, transfer the chicken joints to an ovenproof casserole. Pour juices from the pan over chicken. Add bacon, fried vegetables and prepared bouquet garni. Pour red burgundy over. Cover with a piece of aluminium foil, cook on centre shelf of a moderately slow oven (325 deg. F.—Mark 3) for 1–1¼ hours. Wash mushrooms, then cook in melted butter for 2 minutes. Remove the casserole from oven and fold back aluminium foil. Add mushrooms and cover with foil. Return to oven, continue cooking for 15 minutes. Serve garnished with parsley.

TO PREPARE BOUQUET GARNI:

Place mixed herbs, clove, peppercorns, bay leaf, blade of mace, and parsley stalks in piece of muslin and tie edges securely together.

COOKING WITH WINE

You will perhaps have seen or heard the term 'cooking wine'. Strictly speaking this does not exist. As a guiding rule, if you would hesitate to drink it by the glass then don't use it in your cooking. Your time and effort to prepare a special dish are worthy of the best results possible. On the other hand, don't use an expensive wine as this would lose much of its flavour in cooking. There are many suitable wines at around £1 per bottle.

**Salmon cream
in lemon cups**
page 8

□

Coq au vin

New potatoes

□

Winter fruit salad
page 111

Suggested wine for main course:
Valpolicella

TO FLAMBÉ CHICKEN

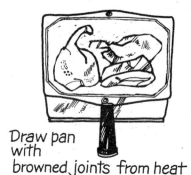

Draw pan
with
browned joints from heat

Pour warmed cognac
evenly over joints
in pan

Set alight
with
match to 'flambé' joints

Chef's specials

Normandy partridge
(*Illustrated left*)

SERVES: TWO

2 young partridges ready for the oven
4 oz. unsalted butter
salt and pepper
2 rashers fat bacon
1½ lb. dessert apples
¼ pint double cream
1½ tablespoons Calvados or brandy

Wipe the partridges. Heat half the unsalted buttered in a flameproof casserole and when really hot brown the partridges all over then sprinkle with salt and pepper. Place bacon over the breasts. Melt remaining butter in another pan and add the dessert apples which have been peeled, cored and cut into wedges. Cover pan closely and cook gently for 5 minutes. Add apples to the casserole. Place in a moderate oven (350 deg. F.— Mark 4) for 20–30 minutes. Transfer to serving dish. Heat the cream and Calvados or brandy together and season to taste. Pour this sauce over the apples in the dish.

Roast partridge

SERVES: FOUR

2 dressed partridges
2 rashers bacon
3–4 oz. butter
little flour
salt and pepper
BROWN GRAVY:
partridge giblets
1 bay leaf
1 clove
6 peppercorns
1 small onion
salt
TO SERVE:
Bread sauce (see p. 188)

Wipe partridges with damp cloth. Place in a meat tin, cover each with a rasher of bacon. Dot with small pieces of butter. Cook on shelf above centre of a moderately hot oven (375 deg. F.—Mark 5) for 30 minutes. Baste occasionally during cooking. Remove partridges from oven, sprinkle with flour and season with salt and pepper. Baste with fat then return to oven for 10 minutes. Transfer partridges to a serving dish, remove bacon and string. Serve with gravy and bread sauce.

TO PREPARE BROWN GRAVY: Place all ingredients in a saucepan. Cover with cold water. Bring to boil and simmer 30 minutes. Drain fat from the tin. Strain stock into meat tin. Bring to boil and boil steadily 5 minutes (do not thicken). Skim before using.

**Tomatoes in
sweet and sour dressing**
page 11

□

Normandy partridge
Buttered potatoes
Peas

□

Lemon soufflé pie
page 115

Suggested wine for main course:
Côte Rôtie

PARTRIDGE

In season from
September Ist February Ist
Best in October

Young birds
require only
3-4 days
hanging

Older birds are best
stewed or braised

Poultry and game menus

Melon and prawn cocktail
page 8

☐

Casserole of duckling
page 77

New potatoes

Green salad
page 98

☐

French apple tart
page 121

Watercress cream soup
page 15

☐

**Roast pheasant with
mushrooms**
page 81

Creamed potatoes

Baby sprouts

☐

Brandied fruit pie
page 107

Salmon cream in lemon cups
page 8

☐

**New England
chicken casserole**
page 72

Boiled rice

☐

Hot apricot slices
page 113

**Tomatoes in
sweet and sour dressing**
page 11

☐

**Roast duckling with
cherry sauce**
page 77

Potato croquettes
page 90

Buttered brussels sprouts

☐

Lemon sorbet
page 119

Cream of cucumber soup
page 17

☐

**Roast duckling with
orange sauce**
page 77

Potato crisps

Buttered potatoes

Garden peas

Watercress

☐

Caramel custard
page 115

Vichyssoise
page 17

☐

Barbecued chicken
page 75

Jacket baked potatoes
page 157—sketch

Simple salad
page 98

☐

Bananas in foil
page 113

Tomatoes Monaco
page 11

☐

**Chicken casserole with
lemon**
page 75

Broccoli

New potatoes

☐

Country house pear pie
page 107

Gazpacho
page 17

☐

Chicken Andalusia
page 75

☐

**Melon with
rich vanilla ice cream**
page 117

Normandy salad
page 11

☐

Chicken with cucumber sauce
page 72

Creamed potatoes

Broccoli

☐

Fruit trifle
page 119

Cream of mushroom soup
page 14

☐

Nutty corn pilaff
page 79

Green salad
page 98

☐

Cherries in wine
page 111

Grilled grapefruit
page 9

☐

Lemon chicken pie
page 73

Creamed potatoes

Braised celery

☐

Meringues Chantilly
page 125

**Tomatoes in
sweet and sour dressing**
page 11

☐

Hunter's casserole
page 81

Jacket baked potatoes
page 157—sketch

Cauliflower

☐

Sunset apples
page 113

Italian tomato cocktail
page 182

☐

**Roast turkey
with all the trimmings**
page 79

Roast potatoes

Buttered sprouts

☐

**Rich and light
Christmas pudding**
page 109

Orange brandy sauce
page 187

Hors-d'œuvre eggs
page 11

☐

Forester's casserole
page 73

Broccoli

Sauté potatoes

☐

Apricot walnut sponge
page 106

Rich custard sauce
page 187

Tomato soup
page 14

☐

**Roast chicken
with celery stuffing**
page 72

Green salad
page 98

☐

Fiesta pancakes
page 106

Watercress cream soup
page 15

☐

Highland grouse
page 81

Potato croquettes
page 90

Brussels sprouts

☐

Chocolate mousse
page 117

6
Vegetables

Scrunchy potatoes (*recipe overleaf*)

Vegetables

Scrunchy potatoes

SERVES: FOUR

1 lb. potatoes
boiling salted water
4–5 oz. butter
2 medium-sized peeled sliced
  onions
4 thick slices white bread
TO SERVE:
1 tablespoon finely chopped
  parsley

Peel the potatoes and cut them into even-sized pieces. Cook in boiling salted water until tender, about 15–20 minutes. Drain well. Meanwhile, melt the butter in a pan. Add the peeled and sliced onions and fry until golden and tender. Remove from pan. Trim crusts from bread. Cut bread into small cubes and fry in remaining butter in pan until golden brown and crisp all over. Remove from pan with draining spoon and drain well on kitchen paper. Add prepared bread cubes and onions to the well-drained potatoes and toss over gentle heat 2–3 minutes. Serve sprinkled with parsley.

Potato croquettes

SERVES: FOUR

2 lb. potatoes
boiling salted water
2 oz. butter or margarine
nutmeg
black pepper
1 egg yolk
1 tablespoon cream
COATING:
2 beaten eggs
6–8 tablespoons browned breadcrumbs
oil or cooking fat for frying

Peel and cut the potatoes into even-sized pieces. Cook in boiling salted water till tender, about 15–20 minutes. Drain well and then stand the pan over a gentle heat for 1–2 minutes to dry the potatoes thoroughly. Mash potatoes well, beat in the butter or margarine, nutmeg and seasoning to taste. Lightly whisk the egg yolk and beat into the potatoes together with cream. Allow to become cold Divide the mixture into twelve and form into croquette shapes with lightly floured hands. Leave for a while in a cool place or refrigerator. Brush with beaten egg and coat in the breadcrumbs. Heat the oil or fat and fry the croquettes till golden brown all over. Drain well and serve immediately.

Vegetable croquettes

SERVES: FOUR TO SIX

1 lb. cold left-over cooked
  potatoes
8 oz. left-over cooked Brussels
  sprouts
4 oz. left-over cooked mashed
  swedes or turnips
1 small onion
1 oz. melted butter
1 tablespoon finely chopped
  parsley
1 tablespoon finely grated
  Parmesan cheese
salt
freshly ground black pepper
1 small beaten egg
COATING:
2 beaten eggs
6–8 tablespoons browned
  breadcrumbs
deep fat for frying

Finely chop potatoes and sprouts, mix with mashed swedes or turnips. Peel and finely chop onion, fry in melted butter till tender but not browned. Add to mixed vegetables, together with parsley, Parmesan cheese, and salt and pepper to taste. Bind together with beaten egg. Form mixture into small balls about the size of a large walnut. Coat vegetable balls in egg and breadcrumbs, fry in hot deep fat for 3–5 minutes till golden brown and crisp. Serve with sliced meat or poultry reheated in rich gravy, or with cold sliced meat, salad and pickles.

DICING VEGETABLES

Peel vegetables and trim into even shape

Cut lengthwise into ¼-½" slices then lengthwise in opposite direction

Slice across into dice with sharp knife

Spinach– Italian style

SERVES: THREE TO FOUR

2 lb. spinach
2 oz. butter
salt and pepper
4 slices boiled ham
FRIED BREAD CUBES:
4 slices bread
oil or cooking fat for frying

Wash the spinach well to remove any grit and strip off any coarse stalks. Pack spinach into a saucepan with only the water left on the leaves. Heat gently, turning occasionally, then bring to boil and simmer until tender, about 8–10 minutes. Drain well. Melt butter in pan and add drained spinach. Season well to taste and stir in chopped ham. Heat together then turn into serving dish and top with fried bread cubes.

TO PREPARE FRIED BREAD CUBES: Trim the crusts from the bread and cut slices into ¼-inch cubes. Melt a little oil or fat in frying pan, then add bread and turn continually until golden brown all over. Drain on absorbent kitchen paper.

Cauliflower crisp

SERVES: FOUR

1 medium-sized cauliflower
boiling salted water
½ pint prepared white sauce (see p. 186)
4 oz. grated Cheddar cheese
salt and pepper
2 tablespoons fresh white breadcrumbs
TO SERVE:
grilled bacon

Trim stalk from cauliflower, divide into flowerets and rinse well in cold water. Place in boiling salted water for 10 minutes until tender but still firm. Drain thoroughly and keep warm in serving dish. Heat prepared white sauce in pan, stirring well. Add grated Cheddar cheese. Season to taste and pour over cooked cauliflower, sprinkle with breadcrumbs. Place in hot oven (400 deg. F.—Mark 6) for 5–10 minutes or until crisp and brown on top. Alternatively place under grill. Top with bacon.

Runner bean hot-pot

SERVES: FOUR TO SIX

1 oz. lard
1 peeled chopped onion
1 clove of garlic
2 rashers chopped de-rinded streaky bacon
2 lb. cooked runner beans
1 lb. small cooked sliced potatoes
salt and pepper
½ pint prepared white sauce (see p. 186)
TO SERVE:
hot crusty French bread

Melt lard in a heavy pan. Add peeled and chopped onion and fry gently until just tender. Crush garlic and add to onion together with chopped, de-rinded bacon. Cook gently for 3–4 minutes. Place a layer of the cooked runner beans in the base of an ovenproof dish, then sprinkle with a little of the fried mixture. Cover with a layer of sliced potatoes. Continue in these layers, seasoning well, finishing with a layer of potatoes. Pour the prepared white sauce over the top and place in a moderate oven (350 deg. F.—Mark 4) for about 30 minutes until hot. Serve with hot crusty French bread.

LATTICED POTATOES

Take peeled potatoes and fluted metal vegetable slice

Cut a thin slice from potato in one direction

Take a thin slice in opposite direction to make lattice

Vegetables

Chicory in cheese sauce

(*Illustrated left*)

SERVES: FOUR

1 lb. chicory
boiling salted water
squeeze of lemon juice
2 chopped hard-boiled eggs (optional)
½ pint prepared Cheese sauce (see p. 186)
1 tablespoon finely grated cheese

Trim off a thin slice from stalk end of chicory and discard, together with any coarse outer leaves. Wash chicory thoroughly in cold water. Cook in boiling salted water with lemon juice for approximately 15 minutes or until tender. Drain well. Arrange in ovenproof dish and, if liked, sprinkle with chopped hard-boiled egg. Pour prepared sauce over and sprinkle with the grated cheese. Brown under a preheated grill until the cheese melts and turns golden brown.

Ratatouille

SERVES: FOUR

2 aubergines
4 courgettes
salt
2 medium-sized onions
2 green peppers
6–8 tablespoons olive oil
1 crushed clove of garlic
8 oz. tomatoes
2 tablespoons chopped parsley
freshly ground black pepper

Cut aubergines and courgettes into ¼-inch slices with stainless steel knife and discard the ends. Sprinkle with salt and leave for at least 30 minutes. Peel and slice onions thinly. Cut a slice from the stalk end of the green peppers, discard seeds and pith. Cut flesh into strips. Heat olive oil and cook onions until tender. Drain any liquid from aubergines and courgettes and add to the pan with sliced peppers and crushed clove of garlic. Cover with a lid and cook over a very gentle heat for 20–25 minutes stirring occasionally until all the vegetables are cooked through. Cut tomatoes into four or eight pieces depending on the size and add to the pan with chopped parsley, salt and freshly ground black pepper. Cover and cook over a gentle heat for further 8–10 minutes. Serve hot or cold.

Red cabbage

SERVES: FOUR TO SIX

1 medium-sized washed drained red cabbage
2 large cooking apples
1 oz. butter
5 tablespoons wine vinegar
3 dessertspoons water
2 oz. granulated sugar
pinch of powdered cloves
salt
freshly ground black pepper
2 large tablespoons redcurrant jelly

Shred the washed and drained red cabbage, discarding any coarse outer leaves. Peel and grate the apples. Place cabbage and apple into a saucepan. Add the butter and shake over very gentle heat until the butter has melted. Add wine vinegar, water, granulated sugar and powdered cloves. Cover with lid. Continue cooking over very gentle heat for 1½–2 hours or until soft. Season with salt and black pepper. Stir in the redcurrant jelly and heat through for a further 5–10 minutes. Serve hot. This can be prepared in advance and reheated when required.

CHOPPING ONION

Cut peeled onion in slices from top to root without cutting through

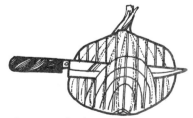

Cut again in thin slices at right angles to other cuts

Turn onion on its side, hold with fork, cut finely

Vegetables

Carrot flan
(*Illustrated left*)
SERVES: SIX TO EIGHT
8 oz. shortcrust pastry (see p. 192)
FILLING:
1 lb. carrots
boiling salted water
1 oz. melted butter
½ pint milk
1 small onion
3 cloves
1 bay leaf
3 eggs
salt and pepper
TO GARNISH:
sprig of parsley

Roll out the pastry and use to line an 11-inch flan ring (see p. 193). Place a 12-inch round of grease-proof paper in flan and fill with baking beans. Bake in hot oven (400 deg. F.—Mark 6) 5–10 minutes. Remove paper and beans, return to oven for 5 minutes or until pastry is cooked. Peel and slice the carrots, cook in boiling salted water for 8 minutes. Drain well, toss in the melted butter, cool slightly. Arrange in overlapping circles in the flan. Heat the milk with onion studded with cloves, add bay leaf, cool, and strain. Beat eggs with strained milk and seasoning. Pour into the flan. Bake above centre in hot oven (400 deg. F.—Mark 6) 25 minutes till egg is set. Serve hot or cold garnished with parsley.

Parsnip chips
SERVES: FOUR
1 lb. parsnips
salt
1–2 oz. plain flour
hot deep fat for frying
1 oz. finely grated Parmesan cheese

Wash, peel and slice the parsnips into chips with a sharp knife (as for potato chips). Soak the chips in cold water for 30 minutes. Place in saucepan with water to just cover. Add salt, bring to the boil and cook for 5 minutes or till just tender. Drain thoroughly, then dry on cloth or absorbent paper and toss in flour. Place parsnip chips in frying basket and lower into hot deep fat and fry 5–8 minutes until crisp and golden brown. If liked sprinkle with finely grated Parmesan cheese. Serve with lamb chops, grilled gammon or fried sausages and bacon.

Baked beetroot in white sauce
SERVES: FOUR
3 uncooked beetroot (approximately 1½ lb.)
½ pint prepared white sauce (see p. 186)
TO GARNISH:
1 chopped spring onion or 1 teaspoon finely chopped chives

Cut off the stalks of the beetroot about 1 inch above the root. Wash carefully without damaging the skin. Wrap in greased greaseproof paper. Place in baking tin in a moderate oven (350 deg. F.—Mark 4), cook until tender, approximately 2 hours. When cooked, allow to cool slightly. Peel away skin and cut into slices or cubes. Coat with freshly prepared white sauce and garnish with chopped spring onion or chives.

USEFUL EQUIPMENT

VEGETABLE RACK
Plastic covered for easy cleaning. Open design allows air to circulate

CHIP PAN: Wire basket converts pan for frying

MANDOLIN: Hold upright, then slice vegetables into fluted or plain slices

7
Salads

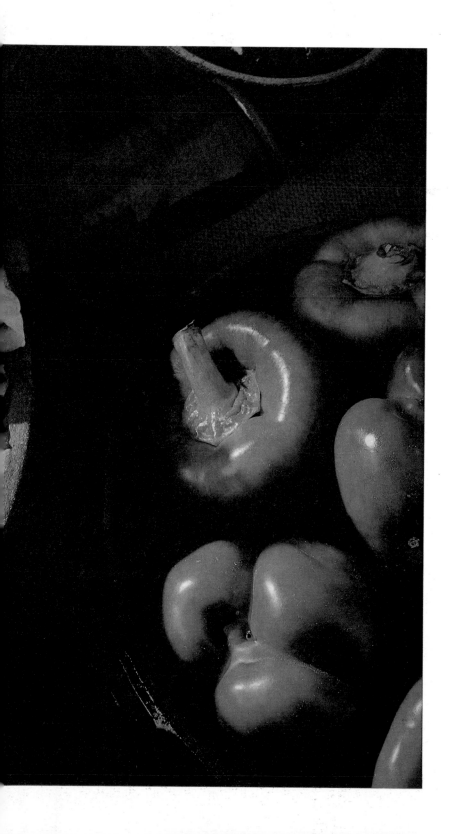

Sunshine salad (*recipe overleaf*)

Salads

Sunshine salad

SERVES: FOUR

4 hard-boiled eggs
1 lettuce
4 firm tomatoes
1 green pepper
1 small onion

TO GARNISH:
12 black olives
6 green olives

TOMATO DRESSING:
½ pint home-made mayonnaise
　(see p. 189)
1 level tablespoon tomato purée
1 level teaspoon paprika pepper

Shell the hard-boiled eggs then cut three in half lengthwise. Chop the remaining egg. Wash and drain the lettuce. Cut each tomato into four to six wedges. Discard the core and seeds from the pepper then cut the green flesh into rings. Peel and slice the onion; separate a few rings for garnish then chop remainder finely. Arrange the prepared lettuce, egg halves, tomato and onion rings attractively in a salad bowl. Mix chopped egg and onion together and place in centre of salad. Top with 3–4 tablespoons tomato dressing just before serving. Garnish with black and green olives. Serve remaining dressing separately.

TO PREPARE TOMATO DRESSING:
Blend mayonnaise with tomato purée. Season with paprika pepper.

Simple salad

SERVES: FOUR

1 cos or round lettuce
2 medium-sized carrots
3 oz. sultanas
French dressing (see p. 189)

Discard any discoloured outer leaves from lettuce. Wash and drain thoroughly and place in serving bowl. Scrape or peel carrots and grate on a coarse grater. Add to lettuce with sultanas. Pour French dressing over salad ingredients just before serving.

This salad can be served as an alternative to a plain green salad.

Green salad

SERVES: FOUR

1 lettuce
1 green pepper
1 small bunch spring onions
1 inch of cucumber
1 small bunch watercress
1 cut clove of garlic (optional)
Garlic French dressing (see p. 189)

Remove any discoloured outer leaves from lettuce, wash and drain thoroughly. If possible leave in a polythene bag in refrigerator for 2–3 hours before serving so that the lettuce will become crisp. Cut a slice from stalk end of green pepper. Scoop out seeds and pith, wash the pepper thoroughly, then slice into rings. Remove outer leaves and roots from spring onions. Trim tops if very long, and chop finely to use in the salad. Wash cucumber and cut into thin slices or cubes. Plunge bunch of watercress into cold water, cut away any stalks or roots and leave to drain. Rub inside of serving bowl with cut clove of garlic if desired. Arrange lettuce, green pepper rings, spring onions and chopped tops, cucumber and watercress attractively in bowl. Pour over Garlic French dressing just before serving and toss lightly.

TOMATO
ROSES

Make eight cuts through skin from top almost to base. Gently separate to form petals.

TOMATO
WATERLILIES

Make zig-zag cuts through centre

Pull apart halves gently

Gina's salad

SERVES: SIX TO EIGHT

1 large lettuce
1 green pepper
2 heads chicory
½ cucumber
3 sticks celery
1 bunch radishes
1 apple
a little lemon juice
6 tomatoes
1 can (7 oz.) sweetcorn kernels
1 bunch watercress
2 oz. raisins
2 oz. salted nuts
double quantity French dressing
(see p. 189)

Wash and drain lettuce thoroughly discarding coarse outer leaves. Cut a slice from stalk end of green pepper, discard seeds and pith and cut flesh into rings. Discard outer leaves and cut chicory into rings. Slice cucumber thinly. Scrub and chop celery. Trim roots and tops from radishes and leave whole or make into radish roses. Wash, core and slice apple. Sprinkle with lemon juice. Cut tomatoes into quarters. Drain sweetcorn kernels. Tear lettuce leaves, place in a large salad bowl, add sprigs of washed watercress and green pepper rings. Add chicory, cucumber, celery and radishes. Mix in apple, tomatoes, sweetcorn, raisins and salted nuts. Pour over prepared French dressing and toss lightly together just before serving.

Salade Niçoise

SERVES: SIX

4 tomatoes
½ small cucumber
½ teaspoon chopped basil
salt and pepper
8 radishes
2 sticks celery
1 green pepper
1 small onion
3 hard-boiled eggs
1 can (7 oz.) tuna fish
1 can (2 oz.) anchovy fillets
1 lettuce
French dressing (see p. 189)
8 black olives

Cut tomatoes into quarters. Thinly slice cucumber. Place in large salad bowl and sprinkle with chopped basil, salt and pepper. Trim radishes and wash well. Scrub and chop celery. Cut a slice from stalk end of green pepper, discard seeds and cut flesh into rings. Peel and thinly slice onion. Shell hard-boiled eggs and cut in quarters. Drain tuna fish. Drain anchovy fillets and cut each in half lengthwise. Tear washed lettuce into small pieces and place in salad bowl with prepared radishes, celery, pepper, onion, eggs and pieces of tuna fish. Pour over French dressing and toss lightly. Garnish with lattice of anchovies. Top with black olives.

Scandinavian cabbage salad

SERVES: THREE TO FOUR

1 lb. red cabbage
6 tablespoons vinegar
salt
freshly ground black pepper
3 tablespoons oil
4 oz. cream or lactic cheese
few chopped chives

Remove any coarse outer leaves from the red cabbage, cut into quarters, discard stem and shred finely. Wash and drain well. Place the cabbage in a large bowl, pour the vinegar over, season well and mix thoroughly together. Leave to stand for 3–4 hours, stirring occasionally. Transfer to serving dish, pour the oil over the cabbage and place teaspoonfuls of cream or lactic cheese on top. Sprinkle with chopped chives. Serve with cold meats.

CELERY CURLS

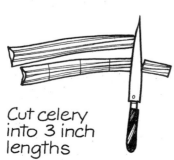

Cut celery into 3 inch lengths

Fringe each end without cutting through centre

Leave to curl in ice-cold water for ½ hour

Salads

Summer salad

(*Illustrated left*)

SERVES: FOUR TO SIX

12 oz. young carrots
1 bunch radishes
½ cucumber
8 oz. Swiss Emmenthal cheese
few lettuce leaves
2 oz. cold cooked meat (optional)
Mint French dressing (see p. 189)

Peel and slice carrots into rings. Remove tops and roots from radishes, then cut into chunky slices. Cut cucumber into ¼-inch slices then into quarters. Trim rind from Swiss Emmenthal cheese, cut into cubes. Wash and drain then shred lettuce leaves. Use most of the lettuce to line base of serving dish. Add all the other ingredients and toss. Top with remaining shredded lettuce. If liked add a few cubes of cold cooked meat. Serve with Mint French dressing.

Coleslaw

SERVES: SIX

½ crisp white cabbage (approximately 1¼ lb.)
2 red dessert apples
a little lemon juice
2 carrots
1 green pepper
1 dessertspoon finely grated onion
½ pint home-made mayonnaise (see p. 189)
salt and pepper
1 oz. coarsely chopped cashew nuts (optional)

Discard the coarse outer leaves from the white cabbage, cut in half and remove the stem. Finely shred the cabbage and place in a bowl of ice-cold water for 30 minutes. Drain thoroughly. Cut red dessert apples into quarters, remove core, chop the flesh and sprinkle with lemon juice. Peel and grate the carrots. Cut green pepper in half, discard stem, seeds and pith, then finely shred the flesh. Place cabbage, apple, carrot and pepper in bowl. Mix the grated onion into the prepared mayonnaise, add to the bowl and toss well. Season to taste. Sprinkle with chopped cashew nuts if liked.

Apple avocado special

SERVES: FOUR

4 red dessert apples
1 avocado pear
juice of 2 lemons
2 oz. mixed salted nuts
bunch watercress
DRESSING:
¼ level teaspoon each salt and pepper
1 teaspoon sugar
2 tablespoons salad oil

Core red dessert apples but do not peel, cut into thin slices. Slice avocado in half, remove stone, peel and cut into thin slices. Cover apple and avocado slices with lemon juice in small bowl to preserve colour. Just before serving drain and keep lemon juice for dressing. Add salted nuts to apple and avocado, toss in prepared dressing, arrange on dish and garnish with washed watercress. Serve with cold chicken or meats.

TO MAKE DRESSING: Mix salt, pepper and sugar with salad oil in small bowl, beat in lemon juice drained from apple and avocado, until well blended.

CARROT CURLS

Cut wafer thin length-wise slices with potato peeler

Roll up slices carefully and secure with cocktail sticks

Leave in ice cold water until crisp. Remove sticks

Salads

Chicken and orange salad

(*Illustrated left*)

SERVES: FOUR TO SIX

6 oz. long grain rice
boiling salted water
½ lb. cooked chicken
2 large oranges
4 oz. Leicester or Cheddar cheese
chopped parsley
DRESSING:
¼ teaspoon salt
freshly ground black pepper
dry mustard
½ teaspoon sugar
1 tablespoon vinegar
3 tablespoons oil

Cook the rice in boiling salted water for 12–15 minutes or until the grains are tender, stirring occasionally with a fork to prevent sticking. Drain through a colander and pour over cold water to keep the grains separate. Allow to become completely cold. Cut the chicken into neat cubes. Peel the oranges and cut each segment in half, removing any pips. Cut Leicester or Cheddar cheese into dice. Mix prepared ingredients in a large salad bowl. Just before serving pour the prepared dressing over and sprinkle with a little chopped parsley.

TO PREPARE DRESSING: Combine all the ingredients together in a screw-top jar and shake until thoroughly combined.

Mixed fish salad

SERVES: FOUR

1 lettuce
1 can (7¾ oz.) salmon
1 can (7 oz.) tuna fish
1 can (4¼ oz.) sardines
1 lemon
PRAWN COCKTAIL:
6 oz. peeled prawns
1 dessert apple
3–4 tablespoons mayonnaise
1 dessertspoon tomato ketchup
salt
freshly ground black pepper

Remove the outer leaves from the lettuce, wash remaining leaves well under running cold water and shake off excess water. Line a platter or large plate with lettuce. Drain excess oil from the salmon and tuna, turn out on to separate plates. Divide into large pieces and remove any skin and bones. Drain oil from sardines. Cut lemon in half, then into thin wedges with a sharp knife. Place prawn cocktail mixture in the centre of the lettuce, then arrange salmon, tuna and sardines round the edge. Place lemon wedges in between each portion of fish.

TO PREPARE THE PRAWN COCKTAIL: Place prawns in a bowl. Dice the dessert apple, removing the core, and add to the prawns. Blend in the mayonnaise and tomato ketchup, then season with salt and freshly ground black pepper.

Apple and herring salad

SERVES: TWO

4 pickled herrings
1 small onion
boiling water
1 red apple
juice of ½ lemon
1 carton (5 oz.) soured cream
salt
freshly ground black pepper
TO GARNISH:
chopped parsley

Drain the pickled herrings and cut each fillet into six to eight strips. Peel and thinly slice onion into rings then place in a bowl and pour over boiling water. Leave for ½ minute and then drain thoroughly and cool. Cut red apple into quarters, core and cut into thin slices. Sprinkle with lemon juice to prevent discoloration. Mix herrings, drained onion rings and apple slices together then add soured cream, salt and black pepper. Chill the salad for 30 minutes if possible, and serve sprinkled with chopped parsley.

USEFUL EQUIPMENT

EGG SLICER

For neat slices of hard boiled egg

SALAD SHAKER

Collapsible, simple to use, easy to store

WOODEN SALAD BOWL

Oil bowl after washing to keep in good condition

Desserts

Puddings and pies
Fruit desserts
Cold sweets
Pastry desserts
Chef's specials

Fiesta pancakes (*recipe overleaf*)

Puddings and pies

Pancakes

MAKES: SIX TO EIGHT

4 oz. plain flour
¼ level teaspoon salt
1 egg
1 egg yolk
½ pint milk
1 tablespoon cooking oil or melted
   butter
oil or fat for frying
TO SERVE:
redcurrant jelly and cream

Sift flour and salt into deep-sided bowl. Hollow out centre, drop in whole egg and egg yolk. Add 2 tablespoons milk, beat with wooden spoon, gradually drawing in flour from sides. Add just over half remaining milk a little at a time, beating well until smooth. Gradually stir in rest of milk and oil or butter. Heat a little oil or fat in a strong frying pan about 7 inches diameter, pour off all but a teaspoon of fat into a small saucepan, keep warm on cooker. Heat fat remaining in frying pan. Pour in 4 tablespoons batter, tilting pan from side to side so base is evenly covered. Cook over quick heat till golden brown underneath, ease round with palette knife, turn pancake over. Cook until golden brown on other side. Make up pancakes with remaining batter in same way. Serve with redcurrant jelly and cream.

Fiesta pancakes

MAKES: SIX TO EIGHT

basic pancake batter (see previous
   recipe)
4 mandarin or seedless oranges
8 maraschino cherries
caster sugar (optional)
SAUCE:
4 oz. cube sugar
strained juice of 1 lemon
¼ pint water

Make up the pancakes as directed in the basic recipe. Roll up pancakes and arrange two on each plate. Pour a little sauce over and decorate with orange segments and maraschino cherries. If liked, sprinkle with a little caster sugar.
TO PREPARE SAUCE: Place the sugar in a strong pan together with the strained lemon juice and water. Stir over a gentle heat until sugar has dissolved, then boil rapidly without stirring until a golden caramel is formed.

Apricot walnut sponge

SERVES: FOUR TO SIX

4 oz. dried apricots
1 oz. walnuts
4 oz. butter or margarine
4 oz. caster sugar
2 lightly beaten eggs
few drops vanilla essence
6 oz. self-raising flour
pinch of salt
2 tablespoons milk
TO SERVE:
hot apricot jam and cream

Wash the dried apricots and cut into small pieces with scissors. Chop the walnuts. Cream the butter or margarine with the sugar until really light and fluffy. Add the lightly beaten eggs a little at a time, beating well after each addition. Beat in vanilla essence. Sift flour and salt together, then fold into creamed mixture alternately with the prepared apricots and walnuts. Stir in the milk without beating. Turn into a well-greased 2-pint ovenproof pie dish and smooth over the top. Bake towards centre of a moderate oven (350 deg. F.—Mark 4) for approximately 1 hour or until well risen and cooked through. Serve with hot apricot jam and cream.

CHOPPING NUTS

Use sharp cook's knife to chop finely

FLAKING ALMONDS

Use sharp vegetable peeler to flake blanched almonds

GRINDING NUTS

Small rotary grinder is ideal for finely grinding

Treacle tart

SERVES: SIX TO EIGHT

12 oz. shortcrust pastry (see p. 192)

FILLING:

3 tablespoons (6 oz.) treacle or golden syrup
1 oz. butter
2 tablespoons milk
finely grated rind and juice of 1 lemon
1 beaten egg
1½ oz. fresh white breadcrumbs
2 oz. sultanas
1 oz. mixed peel

Roll prepared shortcrust pastry on lightly floured board into round to line 9-inch ovenproof pie plate. Trim off surplus pastry, roll out trimmings and cut into shapes. Damp pastry edges and arrange shapes decoratively round the edge. Pour the prepared filling into the pastry case. Bake in the centre of a moderately hot oven (375 deg. F.—Mark 5) for 25–30 minutes or till pastry is cooked through. Serve hot.

TO PREPARE FILLING: Warm the treacle or golden syrup and butter in a bowl over hot water. Remove from heat, add milk, rind and juice of lemon and beaten egg. Mix thoroughly, stir in breadcrumbs, sultanas and mixed peel.

Brandied fruit pie

SERVES: SIX

12 oz. shortcrust pastry (see p. 192)
2 peeled cored sliced cooking apples
beaten egg to glaze
1 tablespoon Demerara sugar

SPICY FILLING:

2 oz. brown sugar
1 oz. butter
½ level teaspoon ground nutmeg
2 oz. stoned raisins
2 oz. currants
2 oz. chopped cherries
3 to 4 tablespoons brandy

Roll out half pastry into round and line a 9-inch ovenproof pie plate. Trim off surplus pastry, roll out remaining pastry into round for lid. Spread half spicy filling over pastry. Cover with peeled, cored and sliced cooking apples. Top with remaining filling. Damp pastry edges, carefully cover with pastry lid, press firmly. Trim edges. Knock up and flute with back of knife. Glaze with half beaten egg. Bake in hot oven (400 deg. F.—Mark 6) 25 minutes. Remove from oven, glaze with remaining beaten egg and sprinkle with Demerara sugar. Return to oven, cook 10 minutes till pastry is golden and the filling cooked.

TO PREPARE SPICY FILLING: Heat brown sugar and butter together until the butter has melted. Add nutmeg, raisins, currants, cherries and brandy. Stir over gentle heat 2 minutes.

Country house pear pie

SERVES: FOUR TO SIX

12 oz. shortcrust pastry (see p. 192)
milk to glaze

FILLING:

1½ lb. cooking pears
2 tablespoons golden syrup
1 level teaspoon ground cinnamon or cloves

Grease a loose-based sandwich tin. Roll out two-thirds of the pastry and use to line base and sides of prepared tin. Trim off surplus pastry with sharp knife. Pile prepared filling in centre. Roll out remaining pastry into round for lid and lift this carefully on top of filling and press down well. Damp top edge with water. Carefully fold over pastry from sides of tin and press down over pastry lid to make a firm seal. Mould a strip of pastry round the handle of a wooden spoon, remove, place in the centre of pie, make small hole in middle of pie for steam to escape. Brush top with milk, then bake just above centre of hot oven (400 deg. F.—Mark 6) for 35–40 minutes until golden brown and cooked through. Lift from sandwich tin on the base and transfer to serving platter. Serve with redcurrant jelly and cream or custard.

TO PREPARE FILLING: Peel, core and slice pears and mix with warmed syrup and cinnamon or cloves.

PASTRY EDGES

Make pattern with teaspoon handle on strip round edge

Overlap squares of pastry round edge. Press down

Twist pastry strip and lightly press on dampened edge

Puddings and pies

Granny's raisin pudding

(*Illustrated left*)

SERVES: FOUR TO SIX

4 oz. plain flour
good pinch of salt
1 level teaspoon baking powder
½ level teaspoon mixed spice
4 oz. fresh white breadcrumbs
3 oz. shredded suet
4 oz. caster sugar
8 oz. Australian stoned raisins
finely grated rind of 1 lemon
1 large or 2 small eggs
6–8 tablespoons milk

TO SERVE:

Syrup sauce (see sketches p. 187)

Grease a 2-pint pudding basin. Sift the flour, salt, baking powder and spice together. Stir in breadcrumbs, shredded suet, caster sugar, Australian stoned raisins and finely grated lemon rind. Beat the egg with a little of the milk and stir into dry ingredients. Add remaining milk if necessary to make soft dropping consistency. Turn into prepared basin. Cover closely with kitchen foil and steam for about 2½ hours or until well risen and cooked through. Serve with Syrup sauce.

Chocolate pudding with fudge sauce

SERVES: SIX

3 oz. plain block chocolate
2 tablespoons milk
6 oz. butter or margarine
6 oz. caster sugar
a few drops vanilla essence
3 whisked eggs
5½ oz. self-raising flour
½ oz. cocoa

FUDGE SAUCE:

8 oz. caramels
¼ pint milk

Grease a 2½-pint pudding basin. Break plain chocolate in small pieces, place with milk in a small pan. Heat gently until melted and smooth. Leave to cool. Cream butter or margarine with caster sugar and vanilla until fluffy. Gradually beat in melted chocolate. Add whisked eggs a little at a time, beating well after each addition. Fold in sifted flour and cocoa. Turn mixture into prepared basin. Cover top closely with double thickness greased greaseproof paper, tie down well, or cover closely with kitchen foil. Place in top of steamer; steam for 2 hours. Remove paper, turn out on hot dish, pour over a little sauce. Serve remaining sauce in a small jug.

FUDGE SAUCE: Place caramels in small pan together with milk, heat slowly until the caramels have dissolved. Stir well, pour into serving jug.

Rich and light Christmas pudding

MAKES: THREE PUDDINGS, EACH SERVING SIX

1 lb. currants
1 lb. sultanas
1 lb. seedless raisins
4 oz. mixed peel
1 lb. butter or margarine
1 lb. dark brown sugar
5 eggs
4 oz. golden syrup
grated rind and juice of 1 lemon
6 oz. self-raising flour
1 teaspoon each mixed spice and nutmeg
1 lb. fresh brown breadcrumbs
1 wineglass rum or brandy
3–4 tablespoons milk

Wash and dry fruits. Finely chop peel. Cream butter or margarine and dark brown sugar together till fluffy. Beat eggs in well. Stir in golden syrup, rind and juice of lemon. Mix in flour sifted with spices. Add breadcrumbs, fruit and peel. Add rum or brandy and milk to blend. Cover bowl, leave to stand overnight. Well grease three 2-pint pudding basins, place round of greased greaseproof paper in base of each. Divide mixture between basins, cover with two thicknesses of greased greaseproof paper and pudding cloth, tie securely. Steam at least 6 hours. Re-cover, re-steam for 2 to 3 hours before serving. Serve with Orange brandy sauce (see p. 187).

COVERING A BASIN

Tear enough kitchen foil to cover basin twice

Hold double thickness of foil over basin with outspread fingers

Press under rim all round to seal completely

Fruit desserts

Cherries in wine

(*Illustrated left*)

SERVES: SIX

2 lb. red cherries
4 oz. granulated sugar
⅛ pint water
½ bottle white wine
1 stick cinnamon

TO SERVE:

Natillas sauce (see p. 187)
  or Ice cream (see p. 117)

Wash the red cherries and remove the stalks. Place granulated sugar and water in a heavy-based saucepan over gentle heat stirring until the sugar has completely dissolved. Allow to come to the boil and boil for approximately 3 minutes to form a thick syrup. Draw from heat and stir in white wine and cinnamon stick. Bring to boil once more, remove cinnamon stick and pour over prepared cherries. (You may like to stone the cherries but it is time-taking.) Allow to stand until completely cold before serving with Natillas sauce or ice cream.

Summer fruit salad

SERVES: FOUR TO SIX

2 dessert pears
3 peaches
strained juice of ½ lemon
1 small fresh pineapple
1 small punnet redcurrants
1–2 tablespoons caster sugar
1–2 tablespoons Kirsch

TO DECORATE:

sprigs of mint

TO SERVE:

cream

Cut dessert pears into quarters and slice thinly. Peel and thinly slice the peaches. Sprinkle pears and peaches with strained lemon juice to preserve the colour. Discard skin and core from the pineapple and cut the flesh into chunks. Wash and pick over the redcurrants. Mix all the prepared fruits together with the caster sugar to taste and Kirsch. Decorate with mint. Chill for 30 minutes. Serve with cream.

Winter fruit salad

SERVES: FOUR

2 dessert apples
2 dessert pears
juice of 1 small lemon
1 orange
2 tablespoons sultanas
3–4 oz. whole dates, stoned
2–3 oz. green grapes
2 oz. hazelnuts

SYRUP:

3 oz. quick-dissolving lump sugar
¼ pint water
1–2 tablespoons brandy (optional)

Peel and core the dessert apples and pears and cut into chunks. Toss in the lemon juice. Prepare orange (see sketches below). Add sultanas, stoned dates, green grapes and hazelnuts and mix well together. Pour the prepared cooled syrup over the top and chill well before serving.

TO PREPARE SYRUP: Place the lump sugar in a pan with water and dissolve over very gentle heat. Bring to the boil without stirring for 2 minutes. Allow to cool, then stir in the brandy if liked.

PEELING ORANGES

Cut orange into quarters, depth of skin only

Remove peel in sections. Cut away white pith

Loosen flesh by cutting into sections between membranes

Fruit desserts

Sunset apples

(*Illustrated left*)

SERVES: SIX

6 even-sized cooking apples
4 oz. stoned raisins
finely grated rind and juice of
  1 lemon
2 oz. soft brown sugar
4–5 tablespoons sieved apricot
  jam

TO DECORATE:

6 teaspoons redcurrant jelly
6 bay leaves

TO SERVE:

Ice cream (see p. 117) or Rich
  custard sauce (see p. 187)

Wash, peel and core cooking apples. Arrange in ovenproof dish. Mix stoned raisins, lemon rind and soft brown sugar together and divide between centres of apples. Sprinkle apples with lemon juice and place a spoonful of apricot jam on top of each. Place in moderate oven (350 deg. F.—Mark 4) until apples are tender, about 45 minutes according to variety and size of fruit. Baste apples with a spoonful of the glaze from the bottom of the dish and decorate top of each with a teaspoonful of redcurrant jelly. Return to oven for further 5 minutes. Decorate with bay leaves. Serve with ice cream or custard.

Hot apricot slices

SERVES: SIX

4 oz. dried apricots
2 tablespoons Demerara sugar
$\frac{1}{4}$ pint water
juice of $\frac{1}{2}$ lemon

PASTRY:

6 oz. self-raising flour
2 oz. fine semolina
4 oz. butter
1 oz. caster sugar
about 1 tablespoon cold water
milk to glaze

TO SERVE:

cream or custard

Snip dried apricots into small pieces with scissors. Cover with water and bring to boil. Drain well then put into pan with Demerara sugar, $\frac{1}{4}$ pint water and lemon juice. Simmer gently until tender, thick and syrupy. Leave to cool.

TO PREPARE PASTRY: Sift flour and semolina then rub in butter finely. Add caster sugar. Mix to a firm dough with water. Knead lightly on floured board till smooth.

TO MAKE UP SLICES: Roll pastry into two rectangles about $9\frac{1}{2}$ by 7 inches. Put one piece on to greased baking sheet and spread with apricot mixture to within 1 inch of edge. Moisten edges with water. Place second piece of pastry on top. Press edges to seal. Brush with milk. Bake towards top of hot oven (400 deg. F.—Mark 6) for 15–20 minutes. Cut in squares. Serve hot with cream or custard.

Bananas in foil

SERVES: FOUR

4 bananas
finely grated rind and juice of 1
  lemon
4 level dessertspoons brown sugar
4 level dessertspoons clear honey
4 level dessertspoons desiccated
  coconut

Peel the bananas and place each one on a square of kitchen foil. Sprinkle each with a little lemon rind and juice, brown sugar and clear honey. Top with desiccated coconut. Pick up edges of foil and fold over to form a seal. Twist the ends to secure. Place in base of a grill pan under a hot grill for 10 minutes, or if the oven is hot, put on a baking sheet and bake for approximately 10 minutes (400 deg. F.—Mark 6). Serve in the foil containers on individual dishes.

SEEDING GRAPES

Sterilize hair grip by plunging in boiling water

Push loop end of grip into grape at stalk end

Pull out pips one at a time

Cold sweets

Lemon soufflé pie

(*Illustrated left*)

SERVES: EIGHT

12 oz. digestive biscuits
3 tablespoons golden syrup
3 oz. butter
12 oz. fresh strawberries
LEMON SOUFFLÉ:
2 egg yolks
6 oz. caster sugar
finely grated rind and
   juice of 2 large lemons
½ pint lightly whipped double
   cream
¼ oz. gelatine
2–3 tablespoons hot water
2 stiffly beaten egg whites

Crush biscuits finely. Melt syrup and butter in large pan. Remove from heat, add biscuits, mix well. Line a 6-inch loose-bottomed cake tin with mixture. Press well into sides and base of tin. Line with half strawberries. Put in cool place or refrigerator 30 minutes.

TO PREPARE LEMON SOUFFLÉ: Place egg yolks, sugar, lemon rind and juice in bowl over pan of boiling water. Whisk until thick and creamy. Remove from pan and whisk 5 minutes until cool. Gently fold in lightly whipped cream. Dissolve gelatine in the hot water, pour in thin stream into mixture, stirring gently. Fold in stiffly beaten egg whites. Pour into prepared tin and leave in cool place or refrigerator. When set slip round-bladed knife gently round sides and ease on to dish. Top with remaining strawberries.

Rich continental cheesecake

SERVES: EIGHT TO TEN

1 packet (7½ oz.) Nice biscuits
4 oz. melted butter
1½ lb. Philadelphia cream cheese
6 oz. caster sugar
2 eggs
1 teaspoon vanilla essence

Place Nice biscuits between two sheets of greaseproof paper. Crush finely with rolling pin. Tip the crumbs into a bowl. Add melted butter and stir until crumbs have absorbed the butter. Press mixture, using the back of a dessertspoon, into a 7–7½-inch loose-bottomed cake tin till the base and halfway up the sides are completely covered. Leave in the refrigerator or a cool place for about 20 minutes. Cream the Philadelphia cheese and caster sugar till well blended. Beat in the eggs one at a time. Beat in vanilla essence. Pour prepared filling into the lined tin. Bake on the centre shelf of a slow oven (300 deg. F.—Mark 2) for 30 minutes till set. Turn off the heat and allow cheesecake to cool in the oven. Remove from the oven and place in refrigerator or cold place overnight. Ease the cheesecake out of the tin and transfer to a plate. Carefully remove the base of the tin using a round-bladed knife. If liked top with fruit, e.g. strawberries, raspberries.

Caramel custard

SERVES: FOUR TO SIX

6 oz. granulated sugar
6 tablespoons water
CUSTARD:
1¼ pints milk
1½ teaspoons vanilla essence
4 oz. caster sugar
5 eggs

Place granulated sugar and water in a heavy-based saucepan. Stir over a gentle heat till sugar has dissolved, then bring to the boil. Boil for about 10 minutes without stirring till liquid turns golden brown in colour. Pour immediately into a 6 inch diameter by 3 inch deep round fixed base cake tin. (See sketches, below.)

TO PREPARE CUSTARD: Heat milk to just below boiling point, do not boil. Stir in vanilla and caster sugar, until sugar has dissolved. Allow to cool for a few minutes. Beat eggs well, then gradually stir in sweetened milk. Strain and pour into caramel-lined cake tin; stand it in a meat tin, filled with warm water to come halfway up the sides of the cake tin. Place on centre shelf of a slow oven (300 deg. F.—Mark 2) for 1¼–1½ hours till custard is set. Remove from the oven, allow to cool. Chill thoroughly in refrigerator, preferably overnight. Carefully slip a knife round the edge of custard to loosen it, then turn on to serving dish.

CARAMEL CUSTARD

Pour prepared caramel into 6 inch cake tin (not loose based)

Hold tin with cloth and rotate until coated all over

Strain prepared custard into caramel lined tin

Cold sweets

Melon with rich vanilla ice cream

(*Illustrated left*)

SERVES: SIX TO EIGHT

4 eggs
2 oz. caster sugar
½ pint milk
few drops vanilla essence
¼ pint single cream
¼ pint double cream
1 melon
8–10 tablespoons Marsala or
    port
6–8 glacé cherries

Turn refrigerator to lowest setting 1 hour before making. Beat 2 whole eggs and 2 egg yolks in a bowl with the caster sugar. Warm the milk and stir into egg mixture with vanilla essence. Stand the bowl over a pan of gently boiling water and cook, stirring, till mixture coats the back of a spoon. Strain into another bowl and cool, whisking occasionally. Whisk the creams until fairly thick and stir into cooled custard. Whisk egg whites stiffly and fold into mixture. Turn into freezing trays and place in freezing compartment of refrigerator for 2 hours or till firm. Wipe melon. Cut in sections and discard seeds. Cut into chunks in large bowl and pour over Marsala or port. Leave 1–2 hours, then divide between serving dishes, reserving some melon for decoration. Spoon ice cream on top. Decorate with remaining melon chunks and glacé cherries.

Chocolate mousse

SERVES: FOUR

4 oz. plain block chocolate
2½ oz. butter
4 eggs
1 tablespoon rum or brandy

Break the plain chocolate into small pieces and place with the butter in a small bowl over a pan of gently steaming water to melt. Then remove bowl from the heat and mix in the egg yolks and rum or brandy. Whisk the egg whites till stiff and standing in peaks and fold into the chocolate mixture. Pour into four individual serving dishes. Leave the mousse to set overnight in a cool place or refrigerator.

VARIATIONS:

Add a little finely grated orange rind when blending in the egg yolks and use Grand Marnier or Cointreau liqueur instead of rum or brandy.

Coffee party mousse

SERVES: FOUR TO SIX

½ oz. powdered gelatine
¼ pint nearly boiling water
3 tablespoons coffee essence
3 eggs
3 oz. caster sugar
¼ pint lightly whipped double
    cream
pinch cream of tartar
TO DECORATE:
8 oz. plain chocolate finger
    biscuits
2–3 tablespoons double cream
8 hazelnuts or walnut halves

Dissolve the gelatine in the hot water, stirring well. Blend in the coffee essence. Leave in a cool place but do not allow to set. Separate the eggs and put yolks with caster sugar into a basin standing over a pan of gently steaming water. Whisk until thick and creamy about 5 minutes. Remove basin from pan and continue whisking until the mixture is cold. Gradually pour in the cooled gelatine, stirring it in gently, fold in cream and cream of tartar. Whisk egg whites stiffly, carefully fold into mixture. Pour into 6-inch fixed base cake tin rinsed out with cold water, leave to set in cool place overnight.
TO DECORATE: Dip cake tin into very hot water and leave for 5 seconds. Immediately invert on to plate, carefully lift off tin. Trim biscuits to same height as mousse, arrange close together all the way round. Decorate with eight whirls of whipped cream and nuts.

MELTING CHOCOLATE

Break chocolate into pieces and place in bowl

Stand bowl over pan of hot water away from heat

Allow to melt, stirring once or twice till smooth

Cold sweets

Strawberry and almond shortcake

(*Illustrated left*)

SERVES: EIGHT TO TEN

8 oz. salted butter
4 oz. caster sugar
8 oz. plain flour
4 oz. ground almonds
few drops almond essence
1 beaten egg white
1–2 oz. caster sugar
2 oz. flaked almonds
1 lb. strawberries
1 pint Rich custard sauce (see p. 187)

Cream salted butter and caster sugar together, add flour gradually together with ground almonds and almond essence. Knead mixture until smooth and free from cracks. Roll mixture out on lightly floured board to form two rounds each approximately 8 inches in diameter. Place in lightly greased 8-inch sandwich tins and smooth tops with a palette knife. Brush tops with beaten egg white and sprinkle with a little caster sugar and flaked almonds. Bake in a moderate oven (350 deg. F.— Mark 4) for 20–30 minutes. Remove from oven, cool on rack. TO ASSEMBLE: Arrange a layer of washed dried strawberries in base of dish. Place round of shortcake on top. Cover with more strawberries, pour over custard, reserving 2 tablespoons for top. Put remaining shortcake in position, spoon custard into middle and decorate with remaining strawberries.

Fruit trifle

SERVES: SIX

1 packet trifle sponges
3 level tablespoons seedless raspberry jam
1 can (1 lb.) pear halves
1 can (15 oz.) raspberries
6 tablespoons sherry
Rich custard sauce (see p. 187)
TOPPING:
½ pint double cream
1 tablespoon caster or icing sugar
sliced and blanched almonds
glacé cherries

Cut sponges in half, spread with raspberry jam and break in pieces into a glass bowl. Drain fruit, reserving syrup; arrange fruit on top of sponges. Take 2 tablespoons pear syrup and 2 tablespoons of raspberry syrup drained from the fruit and blend with the sherry. Pour over sponge and fruit. Chill for 1–2 hours. Spoon custard over top and leave in cool place 12 hours. Whip cream till thick, fold in caster or icing sugar and swirl on top of trifle. Decorate with the sliced blanched almonds and the glacé cherries.

Lemon sorbet

SERVES: SIX

rind and juice of 3 lemons
1 pint cold water
2 rounded teaspoons powdered gelatine
5–6 oz. granulated sugar
4 tablespoons Cointreau (optional)
2 stiffly beaten egg whites

Set refrigerator to coldest setting 1 hour before making. Peel the rind thinly from the lemons. Place the rind in a pan with the cold water, gelatine and sugar. Heat slowly till sugar dissolves then bring to the boil and simmer for 10 minutes in uncovered pan. Strain into a bowl, cool. Add strained lemon juice and turn into refrigerator trays. Chill in freezing compartment of refrigerator until the mixture sets round the edges. Turn into a chilled bowl and whisk till frothy and thick. Whisk in the Cointreau, if using, and the stiffly beaten egg whites. Pour back into the trays and replace in the freezing compartment till firm. Spoon into individual glass dishes. Remember to return refrigerator setting to normal.

LEMON SQUEEZER

EGG SEPARATOR

ROTARY WHISK

Smooth running, efficient whisk

Easy to clean lemon squeezer. Container for juice beneath

Aluminium egg separator ensures success every time

Pastry desserts

French apple tart

(*Illustrated left*)

SERVES: EIGHT TO TEN
1 lb. prepared puff pastry
1½ lb. cooking apples
lemon juice
caster sugar
3 oz. butter
APRICOT GLAZE:
6 tablespoons apricot jam
3 tablespoons water
1 tablespoon brandy (optional)

Divide pastry in half. Roll each into an oblong about 13–14 inches long by 4–5 inches wide. Trim edges with a sharp knife. Transfer each pastry oblong to a damp baking sheet. Roll out any trimmings and left-over pastry into long strips. Brush edges of pastry with water. Lay strips down each long side. Knock up and flute the edges with a round-bladed knife making a very neat 'well'. Peel, core and quarter the apples. Slice each quarter thinly. Sprinkle with lemon juice. Arrange slices in overlapping rows on pastry. Dust the apples well with caster sugar and dot with pieces of butter. Bake on shelf above centre of a hot oven (400 deg. F.—Mark 6) for 25–35 minutes till cooked through. Coat with prepared apricot glaze.

TO PREPARE APRICOT GLAZE: Heat apricot jam and water in a small saucepan, stirring constantly. Strain through a sieve. Stir in brandy, if using, and keep warm until required.

Danish hazelnut dessert

SERVES: SIX
3 oz. hazelnuts
6 oz. plain flour
salt
4 oz. butter
2½ oz. caster sugar
1 egg yolk
1 can (1 lb. 13 oz.) sliced peaches
¼ pint double cream
¼ pint single cream
a little sifted icing sugar

Lightly toast hazelnuts, remove skins and grind finely. Sift flour and salt into a mixing bowl, make a well in the centre. Add butter, sugar, egg yolk and nuts and bind ingredients together. Chill mixture in refrigerator for 30 minutes, then divide it into three pieces, roll each piece into a round 6–6½ inches in diameter. Carefully transfer to baking trays. Bake pastry rounds on shelf below top of a moderate oven (350 deg. F.—Mark 4) for 15 minutes till pale golden. Place cooked pastry on cooling rack. Drain peaches and arrange half of them on one cooled pastry round. Whip creams together and use half of them to cover peaches. Place second pastry round on top, cover with remaining peaches and cream. Top with third pastry round. Dredge with icing sugar.

Tarte à l'orange

SERVES: EIGHT TO TEN
PASTRY
8 oz. plain flour
pinch of salt
5 oz. butter
1 oz. caster sugar
2 egg yolks
a little cold water if necessary
FILLING:
1 egg
5 oz. sugar
juice and finely grated rind of 1 large orange
2 oz. melted butter

TO PREPARE PASTRY: Sieve the flour and salt into a mixing bowl. Add the butter cut into small pieces then rub in finely. Add the caster sugar to the egg yolks and mix lightly together. Make a well in centre, add eggs and mix to form firm paste. Add water if necessary. Leave for short time. Line a 10-inch shallow flan ring with prepared pastry, trim off surplus. Pour in the prepared filling. Roll out the remaining pastry and cut into strips, then arrange in a lattice pattern over the top. Bake just above centre of a hot oven (425 deg. F.—Mark 7) for about 25 minutes.

TO PREPARE FILLING: Beat all the ingredients together until well blended.

SKINNING HAZELNUTS

Spread hazelnuts out on baking tray or roasting tin

Set in moderate oven (350-F Mark 4) for 10 minutes

Rub briskly in clean teatowel or cloth to remove skins

Chef's special

Lemon meringue pie
(*Illustrated left*)

SERVES: SIX

ALMOND CRUST:

9 oz. plain flour
3 oz. ground almonds
¼ teaspoon salt
6 oz. butter or margarine
3 oz. caster sugar
1 beaten egg

FILLING:

2 oz. cornflour
just under ¾ pint water
¼ level teaspoon salt
1 oz. butter
rind and juice of 1 large or 2
    small lemons
2 egg yolks
3–4 oz. sugar

MERINGUE:

2 egg whites
4 oz. caster sugar

TO DECORATE:

glacé cherries and angelica
caster sugar for dredging

TO PREPARE ALMOND CRUST: Sift flour, ground almonds and salt together. Rub in butter or margarine until like fine breadcrumbs then stir in caster sugar. Bind pastry to a firm dough with beaten egg. Knead lightly and set aside in a cool place or refrigerator for about 30 minutes before using. Carefully roll out prepared almond crust into a round large enough to line an 8-inch fluted flan ring set on a baking sheet. Ease the pastry into the flan ring with fingers so that the edge is even in thickness. Roll rolling pin over the top of the flan and remove any excess pastry. Place a 10-inch round of grease-proof paper in the flan and weigh down with baking beans. Cook in a moderately hot oven (375 deg. F.—Mark 5) for 15 minutes to set the pastry, then remove the paper and the beans. Return flan case to oven for further 5 minutes to cook the pastry. Fill with prepared lemon filling and return to oven for further 10–15 minutes or until filling has set. Pile prepared meringue topping on lemon filling, decorate with glacé cherries and angelica then dredge with caster sugar. Return to moderate oven (350 deg. F.—Mark 4) to lightly brown 5 minutes. Serve hot or cold.

TO PREPARE FILLING: Blend cornflour with a little of the water till smooth. Heat remaining water, salt, butter, lemon rind and juice in pan until boiling, then pour over blended cornflour stirring all the time. Return to pan and cook over gentle heat for about 5 minutes stirring continuously. Remove from heat, cool slightly then beat in egg yolks and sugar.

TO PREPARE TOPPING: Whisk egg whites till stiff. Add 2 teaspoons caster sugar and whisk again till holding its shape. Carefully fold in remaining sugar with metal spoon.

ZigZag Melon
sketches page 8

□

Chicken Andalusia
page 75

Green salad
page 98

□

Lemon meringue pie

Suggested wine for main course:
Piesporter Michelsberg

CHOCOLATE PIE FILLING

Make filling as for lemon meringue pie but omit lemon

Melt 4 oz chocolate in bowl over pan of hot water

Add chocolate at same time as egg yolks and sugar

Chef's special

Meringues Chantilly
(*Illustrated left*)
MAKES: EIGHT
4 egg whites
8 oz. caster sugar
¼ pint piped whipped double
  cream
TO DECORATE:
few pieces of glacé cherries
leaves of angelica

Line baking trays with non-stick vegetable parchment or lightly greased greaseproof paper. Whisk egg whites until they are stiff. Add 4 teaspoons of caster sugar and whisk again until smooth and satiny. Whisk in half the remaining sugar, then fold in rest of sugar with a metal spoon, quickly and lightly. Use 2 tablespoons to shape the mixture into neat shapes on lined baking trays. Bake in coolest oven possible (225 deg. F.—Mark ¼) for about 2–3 hours or until meringues are set. Carefully transfer to wire racks and allow to cool. Sandwich meringues together with piped whipped double cream. Decorate with pieces of glacé cherries and angelica leaves.

VARIATIONS ON SERVING MERINGUES
Try these other delicious ways of serving meringues.

1. FRUIT FILLING: Sandwich prepared meringues together with a slice of a canned pear half. Serve with cream.

2. MERINGUE GLACÉ: Sandwich prepared meringues together with a slice of coffee ice cream. Decorate with piped whipped cream and angelica.

3. MACAROON FILLING: Fold 1 lightly crushed macaroon into ¼ pint whipped double cream. Sandwich prepared meringues together with this. Decorate with split blanched almonds.

Grilled grapefruit
page 9

□

Savoury roast pork
page 40

Scrunchy potatoes
page 90

Red cabbage
page 93

□

Meringues Chantilly

Suggested wine for main course:
**Châteauneuf-du-Pape
red or white**

MERINGUE SHELL

Mark circle on oiled
grease proof paper
on baking sheet

Spread ⅓ meringue
mixture on circle

Place
remainder
in forcing
bag

Build up sides of
meringue to make wall

9
Cakes and Bakes

Individual cakes
Family cakes
Bread and scones
Biscuits and cookies
Chef's specials

Frangipan tartlets (*recipe overleaf*)

Individual cakes

Frangipan tartlets

MAKES: EIGHT

6 oz. shortcrust pastry (see p. 192)

FILLING:

4 oz. butter or margarine

4 oz. caster sugar

1 large lightly whisked egg

4 oz. ground almonds

1 oz. sifted plain flour

1 dessertspoon lemon juice

TOPPING:

2–3 oz. flaked almonds

2 tablespoons warmed sieved apricot jam

8 glacé cherries

Roll out prepared pastry on a lightly floured board. Cut into 4-inch rounds with a plain cutter, use to line eight individual patty tins. Prick base lightly with a fork. Place teaspoonfuls of the prepared filling into cases. Sprinkle top with flaked almonds. Bake in a moderately hot oven (375 deg. F.—Mark 5) for 20–25 minutes or until filling is cooked and almonds lightly browned. Remove from the oven and carefully transfer to a wire rack. While still warm brush tops with apricot jam and decorate with glacé cherries.

TO PREPARE FILLING: Cream butter or margarine with caster sugar. Gradually beat in lightly whisked egg. Fold in ground almonds, sifted flour and lemon juice.

Jap cakes

MAKES: EIGHT

3 egg whites

6 oz. caster sugar

6 oz. ground almonds

2 oz. chopped walnuts

COFFEE BUTTER CREAM:

3 oz. butter or margarine

5–6 oz. sifted icing sugar

1 dessertspoon coffee essence

TO DECORATE:

chocolate buttons

Line a greased shallow oblong baking tin with greased greaseproof paper. Whisk egg whites until very stiff, fold in caster sugar and ground almonds as lightly as possible. Spread mixture in prepared tin and bake in moderate oven (350 deg. F.—Mark 4) for about 30 minutes or until just set. Remove from oven and cut into 1½- or 2-inch rounds with pastry cutter, keeping trimmings. Return rounds and trimmings to oven for a few minutes to brown lightly. Remove rounds, cool on rack; allow trimmings to continue cooking until crisp and brown, then crush with a rolling pin. Sandwich rounds together in pairs with coffee butter cream. Spread sides and top of each cake with butter cream and roll in crushed crumbs and chopped walnuts. Decorate with butter cream and chocolate buttons.

TO PREPARE COFFEE BUTTER CREAM: Cream butter or margarine lightly, then beat in sifted icing sugar until light and fluffy. Add coffee essence.

Iced cakelets

Basic sandwich cake mixture (see Coffee House Gâteau, p. 143) baked in oblong tin approximately 11 by 7 by 1½ inches.

APRICOT GLAZE:

4 tablespoons apricot jam

2 tablespoons water

GLACÉ ICING:

8 oz. icing sugar

3–4 teaspoons warm water

colouring and essence

TO DECORATE:

mimosa balls

small pieces of angelica

assorted vegetable colourings

crystallized rose petals

small pieces chocolate flake bar

Trim the edges then cut the cooled cake into a selection of shapes with a sharp knife or biscuit cutter. For example, six 1½-inch squares, six 1½ by 2½-inch oblongs, six 1½-inch rounds. Glaze and ice cakes (see sketches below). Decorate.

TO PREPARE APRICOT GLAZE: Heat the jam and water together then pass through a sieve and use while hot.

TO PREPARE GLACÉ ICING: Sift icing sugar into a bowl. Add water gradually and beat with a wooden spoon until creamy consistency. Add a few drops of colouring or essence to taste.

ICING CAKELETS

Place cakelets on wire rack, brush with apricot glaze

Spoon to cover, using various colours of glacé icing

When icing has nearly set, arrange decorations on top

Picnic slices

MAKES: ABOUT SIXTEEN SLICES
8 oz. block milk chocolate
2 oz. butter or margarine
4 oz. caster sugar
1 beaten egg
4 oz. desiccated coconut
2 oz. sultanas
2 oz. glacé cherries, quartered

Break milk chocolate into pieces and melt in basin over pan of hot water. Pour into bottom of greased swiss roll or oblong shallow tin approximately 11 by 7 inches, and allow to set. Cream butter or margarine and sugar until light and fluffy. Add beaten egg, then desiccated coconut, sultanas and quartered cherries. Mix well and spread out evenly over the set chocolate. Bake in slow oven (300 deg. F.—Mark 2) for approximately 45 minutes until golden brown. Take out of oven and after 5 minutes mark into slices, then leave until quite cold. Lift the slices out of the tin.

Cherry fancies

MAKES: SIXTEEN
8 oz. butter or margarine
2 oz. sifted icing sugar
a few drops vanilla essence
8 oz. plain flour
2–3 oz. halved glacé or maraschino cherries
GLAZE:
2–3 tablespoons apricot jam
1 dessertspoon water

Cream the butter or margarine and sifted icing sugar till light and fluffy. Add vanilla essence. Sift the flour and add half to the creamed mixture. Beat well then stir in remaining sifted flour and mix well. Place the mixture into a forcing bag fitted with a small vegetable star pipe. Start piping from the centre of non-stick patty tins in a spiral to form a case. Leave for at least 30 minutes in a refrigerator or a very cold place before baking, then place in a slow oven (300 deg. F.—Mark 2) for ¾–1 hour or till pale golden in colour and cooked through. After 5 minutes remove carefully from tins and leave on wire rack to cool completely. (These can be made in advance and when cold stored in airtight tin.) Fill centre of tarts with halved glacé or maraschino cherries. Spoon a little prepared glaze over each and serve.

TO PREPARE GLAZE: Heat sieved apricot jam and blend with water.

Pineapple creams

MAKES: TWELVE
6 oz. shortcrust pastry (see p. 192)
1 can (12 oz.) pineapple pieces
¼ pint double cream
6 oz. sifted icing sugar
yellow colouring
TO DECORATE:
glacé cherries
angelica

Roll pastry to ¼ inch thick. Cut out circles with pastry cutter and use to line twelve greased deep patty tins. Prick base of pastry well with fork and bake 'blind' in hot oven (400 deg. F.—Mark 6) for about 20–25 minutes until cooked through and pale golden. Allow to cool on wire rack. Drain the pineapple pieces, chop coarsely and arrange a little in the base of each pastry case. Whip the cream until thickened and put a good teaspoonful on top of pineapple. Spread lightly with a knife to make a fairly smooth surface. Blend sifted icing sugar with a little pineapple juice to a thick creamy consistency and mix in a few drops yellow colouring. Coat the top of each pastry in turn by carefully spreading a teaspoonful pineapple icing over the cream so that it is completely covered. Decorate with small pieces of glacé cherry and angelica and leave in a cool place until set.

CUTTING ANGELICA

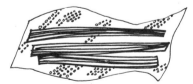

Pour boiling water over angelica strip. Drain and dry well

Cut into ¼–½ inch strips, then diagonally into diamonds

Alternatively, narrow strips may be cut into ½ inch length spikes

Family cakes

Cumberland cutting cake

(*Illustrated left*)
12 oz. plain flour
1 rounded teaspoon mixed spice
pinch of salt
6 oz. lard
6 oz. caster sugar
6 oz. currants
6 oz. sultanas
3 level teaspoons bicarbonate of
    soda
8 fluid oz. milk

Grease and line 2 lb. loaf tin with greased greaseproof paper. Sift flour, mixed spice and salt into a large bowl. Rub in lard with fingertips until like breadcrumbs then stir in caster sugar, currants and sultanas. Dissolve bicarbonate of soda in milk then stir into dry ingredients. Beat thoroughly then turn into prepared tin. Leave in a cool place or refrigerator overnight. Bake towards centre of a moderate oven (350 deg. F.— Mark 4) for approximately 2–2½ hours or until well risen and cooked through when tested with a skewer. If the top browns too quickly cover with a sheet of greaseproof paper. Allow the cake to cool in tin, then strip off paper and store in an airtight tin until required. This cake keeps well.

Keep-if-you-can cake

(*No eggs needed*)
3 oz. glacé cherries
1 lb. plain flour
1 level teaspoon salt
8 oz. caster sugar
6 oz. margarine
8 oz. currants
6 oz. sultanas
4 oz. seedless raisins
4 oz. chopped mixed peel
2 level teaspoons bicarbonate of
    soda
½ pint milk
3 tablespoons malt vinegar

Grease and line an 8-inch round by 3-inch deep cake tin with greased greaseproof paper. Cut the glacé cherries into quarters. Sift the flour with salt into mixing bowl. Stir in caster sugar. Add margarine and rub in finely. Add cleaned fruits, glacé cherries and chopped mixed peel. Dissolve the bicarbonate of soda in the milk, add the malt vinegar, then beat quickly into the dry ingredients until smooth. Transfer to prepared tin and smooth top with knife. Bake in centre of moderate oven (350 deg. F.—Mark 4) about 2¾ hours or till cooked through. Cover with double sheet of greaseproof paper for the last hour to prevent over-browning. Allow to cool in tin 4–5 minutes, then turn out on to cooling tray. Store in airtight tin for a few days before cutting.

Golden honey cake

4 oz. butter or margarine
4 oz. caster sugar
3 whisked eggs
2 tablespoons clear honey
8 oz. sifted self-raising flour
pinch of salt
milk to moisten

Line a 7-inch round cake tin with greased greaseproof paper. Cream butter or margarine with caster sugar until light and fluffy. Gradually beat in the whisked eggs and the clear honey with a little of the sifted flour and pinch of salt. Fold in the remaining sifted flour with sufficient milk to make a soft dropping consistency. Turn into prepared tin and bake in centre of a moderate oven (350 deg. F.— Mark 4) for about 1 hour or until golden and cooked through. Cool and serve cut into slices. Spread with butter if liked.

LINING A CAKE TIN

Cut two rounds plus band of greaseproof paper to fit tin. Brush tin with oil

Fold ½ inch paper along band. Cut every ½ inch. Fit in one round

Fit band, cover with other round, brush again with oil

Family cakes

Dundee cake
(*Illustrated left*)
11 oz. plain flour
pinch of salt
8 oz. butter
grated rind of 1 lemon
8 oz. caster sugar
4 eggs
8 oz. sultanas
8 oz. currants
3 oz. chopped mixed peel
3 oz. ground almonds
2 tablespoons sherry or milk
3 oz. split almonds
a little milk for brushing

Grease and line a 9-inch round by 3-inch deep cake tin with greased greaseproof paper. Sift the flour and salt on a piece of paper. Cream the butter, lemon rind and caster sugar well together till light and fluffy. Gradually beat in the eggs one at a time, beating well after each addition. Fold in half the flour and then the sultanas, currants, chopped mixed peel and ground almonds. Fold in the remaining flour and the sherry or milk. Turn into the prepared tin and smooth the top. Arrange the split almonds over the cake and brush with a little milk. Bake in the centre of a moderate oven (350 deg. F.—Mark 4) for 2 hours until firm to the touch. Turn on to a wire tray, remove paper and allow to cool. Store in airtight tin a few days before using.

White ginger loaf
8 oz. plain flour
1 level teaspoon baking powder
¼ level teaspoon ground ginger
6 oz. butter or margarine
6 oz. caster sugar
3 whisked eggs
4 oz. chopped preserved ginger
ICING:
8 oz. icing sugar
1 tablespoon ginger syrup
1–2 tablespoons hot water
TO DECORATE:
1–2 pieces of preserved ginger

Grease and line a 2 lb. loaf tin. Sift dry ingredients into bowl. Cream butter or margarine and caster sugar together till light and fluffy. Gradually beat in whisked eggs. Fold in sifted dry ingredients. Stir in well chopped preserved ginger. Turn into prepared tin. Bake towards centre in moderately slow oven (325 deg. F. —Mark 3) for 1¼–1½ hours or till cooked through. Cool on wire rack and remove paper. Pour prepared icing over cake when cool. Decorate with slices of preserved ginger.
TO PREPARE ICING: Sift icing sugar into bowl. Add 1 tablespoon ginger syrup and 1–2 tablespoons hot water. Beat till smooth coating consistency.

Auntie Flo's chocolate cake
4 oz. butter or margarine
4 oz. caster sugar
3 eggs
2½ oz. self-raising flour
4 oz. powdered drinking chocolate
½ level teaspoon baking powder
CHOCOLATE ICING:
4 oz. sifted icing sugar
1 dessertspoon sifted cocoa powder
½ oz. butter
1–2 tablespoons hot water
TO DECORATE:
6–7 walnuts

Grease and line a 7-inch round cake tin with greased grease-proof paper. Cream butter or margarine and caster sugar together till light and fluffy. Beat in eggs one at a time, beating well after each addition. Sift dry ingredients together, fold into creamed mixture. Turn into cake tin, smooth over top. Bake on middle shelf of moderate oven (350 deg. F.—Mark 4) 1 hour or till firm to touch. Cool in tin 10 minutes, turn out, cool on wire rack. Spread with icing, decorate with walnuts.
TO PREPARE ICING: Place sifted icing sugar and cocoa in basin over pan of hot water to heat. Remove from heat, add butter and water, beat until smooth.

BLANCHING ALMONDS

Pour boiling water over almonds. Leave for 10 minutes

Pinch between thumb and fingers to work skin off

Use sharp knife or thumb nail to split in half lengthwise

Family cakes

Wholewheat gingerbread

(*Illustrated left*)

4 oz. plain flour
pinch of salt
1 level teaspoon mixed spice
3 level teaspoons ground ginger
4 oz. wholewheat flour
1½ oz. Demerara sugar
1½ oz. sultanas
1½ oz. chopped mixed peel
4 oz. butter or margarine
4 oz. golden syrup
4 oz. black treacle
1 level teaspoon bicarbonate of
    soda
½ pint warm milk
1 beaten egg
1 oz. split almonds

Grease and line an oblong baking tin, about 6 by 9 inches. Sift plain flour, salt, mixed spice and ground ginger into a mixing bowl. Stir in wholewheat flour, Demerara sugar, cleaned sultanas and mixed peel. Place butter or margarine into a bowl with golden syrup and black treacle and heat over a pan of hot water until melted. Add to dry ingredients, beat well. Dissolve bicarbonate of soda in warm milk and add beaten egg. Pour into prepared mixture and beat to form a smooth batter. Pour into tin. Scatter almonds over top, bake in centre of moderate oven (350 deg. F.—Mark 4) for 40–45 minutes until well risen and springy to touch. Cool slightly in tin, then turn on to wire tray, remove paper. Store in airtight tin for 2–3 days before cutting.

Fruity malt loaf

8 oz. wholemeal flour
3 level teaspoons baking powder
pinch of salt
3 oz. malt extract
2 oz. soft brown sugar
1 oz. butter
8 tablespoons water
2 oz. currants
2 oz. sultanas
1 oz. chopped candied mixed
    peel

Sieve dry ingredients together into a mixing bowl. Heat malt extract, soft brown sugar, butter and water gently together in saucepan until dissolved then allow to cool a little. Make a well in the centre of the dry ingredients then pour in the liquid. Add the fruits and chopped candied mixed peel and mix together until blended. Turn into a well-greased and floured 1 lb. loaf tin. Bake in a moderately slow oven (325 deg. F.—Mark 3) for 1¼–1½ hours until springy to touch. Store at least 1 day in airtight tin, then serve with butter.

Date loaf

2–3 oz. flaked almonds
7 oz. dates
4 eggs
7 oz. caster sugar
5 oz. sifted plain flour
7 oz. ground almonds
TO DECORATE:
a few glacé cherries

Grease a 2 lb. loaf tin and line base with greased greaseproof paper. Sprinkle with a few of the flaked almonds. Remove stones from dates and cut fruit into small pieces. Separate whites from yolks of eggs. Beat egg yolks and caster sugar together in a bowl over pan of hot water till thick and creamy. Fold in sifted flour, ground almonds and chopped dates. Whisk egg whites till stiff and standing in peaks, and carefully fold into mixture. Turn into prepared tin, cover with the remaining flaked almonds, bake in moderate oven (350 deg. F.—Mark 4) for 1¾–2 hours or till cooked through and almonds nicely browned on top. Leave for a few minutes before removing from tin, carefully strip off paper when cool and decorate with glacé cherries. Slice to serve.

SIMPLE
CAKE DECORATION

Choose a doily with pretty open design

Place on top of cake and dust with icing sugar

Lift off doily with definite upwards movement

Bread and scones

Cottage loaf
(*Illustrated left*)
MAKES: 3-LB. LOAF
2 lb. plain flour
2 level teaspoons sugar
2 rounded teaspoons dried yeast
16 fluid oz. lukewarm milk
2 beaten eggs
6 tablespoons cooking oil
2 level teaspoons salt

Sift 10 oz. of the flour into a mixing bowl. Add sugar, yeast and lukewarm (not hot) milk. Mix well then leave in a warm place for about 20 minutes till frothy. Add beaten eggs, oil, remaining sifted flour and salt. Beat well. Turn dough on to a lightly floured board and knead and stretch well for 10 minutes till the dough is elastic and no longer sticky. Shape into neat round, place in an oiled polythene bag. Loosely tie bag and place in a bowl. Allow to rise in warm place for $\frac{3}{4}$–1 hour till dough doubles its size and springs back when pressed. To shape dough, see sketches below. Cover with a damp cloth then leave to prove in a warm place for 20–30 minutes. Dust loaf with flour and bake on centre shelf of a very hot oven (450 deg. F.—Mark 8) for 25–35 minutes till golden brown and crusty. When cooked, loaf should sound hollow if tapped on base. Place on wire rack to cool.

Raisin loaves
MAKES: TWO SMALL LOAVES
risen dough (see previous recipe)
8 oz. seedless raisins
clear honey to glaze

Make dough following instructions in previous recipe. After it has risen work the raisins into the dough by squeezing with one hand till thoroughly mixed. Divide dough into two pieces and shape them into neat rounds. Allow to prove in a warm place as in previous recipe. Bake on centre shelf of a very hot oven (450 deg. F.—Mark 8) for approximately 20 minutes. If liked, brush tops of hot loaves with wet brush dipped in clear honey.

Cheese loaf
MAKES: ONE SMALL LOAF
8 oz. self-raising flour
$\frac{1}{2}$ level teaspoon dry mustard
pinch of cayenne pepper
$\frac{1}{2}$ level teaspoon onion or celery salt
2 oz. butter or margarine
4 oz. finely grated cheese
1 beaten egg made up to $\frac{1}{4}$ pint with milk

Lightly grease a 2-lb. loaf tin. Sift the flour, mustard, cayenne pepper and onion or celery salt into a bowl. Add the butter or margarine and rub in to resemble fine breadcrumbs. Stir in the grated cheese. Mix to a firm dough with the beaten egg and milk, using a knife. Turn on to a lightly floured board and knead gently till smooth. Form the dough into a roll the length of the prepared tin, place in the tin and push out to fit evenly. Bake above centre in a moderately hot oven (375 deg. F.—Mark 5) for 35–45 minutes till golden and cooked and the loaf sounds hollow when tapped on the base. Cool on a wire tray. Serve cut into slices and butter well. Best served on day it is made.

SHAPING COTTAGE LOAF

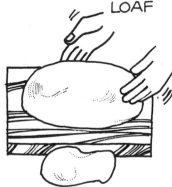

Cut off $\frac{1}{3}$ dough. Shape larger piece into neat round. Place on baking tray

Shape remainder into smaller round fit on top

Press handle of floured wooden spoon through centre

Bread and scones

Devonshire splits
(*Illustrated left*)

MAKES: TWENTY-FOUR

12 oz. self-raising flour
pinch of salt
4½ oz. margarine
3 oz. caster sugar
about 4 tablespoons milk

TO SERVE:

3 tablespoons strawberry jam
4 oz. Devonshire clotted cream
  or ¼ pint whipped double
  cream

Sift flour and salt into a bowl, rub in margarine with the fingertips till mixture resembles fine breadcrumbs. Stir in caster sugar, mix to a stiff dough with the milk. Knead until smooth and free from cracks. Roll out dough to ½–¾ inch thick on a lightly floured board. Cut into 2½-inch rounds. Place on a greased baking tray and bake on shelf above centre of a hot oven (400 deg. F.—Mark 6) for about 10–15 minutes till well risen and cooked through. Transfer to a wire rack, allow to cool. Split or cut in half, serve with strawberry jam and Devonshire clotted or whipped double cream.

Brown soda bread

MAKES: ONE SMALL LOAF

6 oz. plain flour
1 level teaspoon salt
1½ level teaspoons bicarbonate of
  soda
3 level teaspoons cream of tartar
¼ oz. sugar
6 oz. wholemeal flour
about 8 fluid oz. milk or milk
  and water mixed

Sift plain flour, salt, bicarbonate of soda, cream of tartar and sugar into bowl. Add wholemeal flour, mix to soft dough with the milk or milk and water mixed, using a knife. Turn on to floured board and shape into a flat round, about 1 inch thick. Heat a griddle, heavy frying pan or electric hotplate and grease lightly. Place the dough on the heated griddle and cut into quarters. Lower the heat and cook for about 10 minutes till brown on the underside. Turn each piece and cook gently till golden brown and cooked through, about 30–40 minutes.

Drop scones

MAKES: APPROXIMATELY EIGHTEEN

5 oz. plain flour
2 level teaspoons baking powder
pinch of salt
1 level tablespoon caster sugar
1 oz. melted butter or oil
1 beaten egg
¼ pint milk

TO SERVE:

butter
jam or honey

Sift the flour, baking powder and salt into a bowl. Mix in the caster sugar and make a well in the centre. Add the melted butter or oil and beaten egg and mix to a smooth batter, gradually adding the milk. Heat a heavy frying pan or griddle and grease very lightly. Pour tablespoonfuls of the mixture from the point of the spoon to give round flat cakes. As soon as the drop scones are puffed up and bubbles burst on the surface and the underside is golden brown, turn and cook on the other side until browned and cooked through. Serve immediately or place between a folded napkin or a teatowel till required. Serve with butter and jam or honey.

DROP SCONES

Pour batter from point of spoon to give rounds

When surface is full of bubbles, turn with palette knife

When cooked through, place between folds of teacloth

Biscuits and cookies

Viennese orange shortcakes
(*Illustrated left*)
MAKES: TWELVE TO FOURTEEN
4 oz. table margarine
3 oz. butter
3 oz. sifted icing sugar
finely grated rind of 2 oranges
½ oz. sifted cornflour
4 oz. sifted self-raising flour
4 oz. sifted plain flour
icing sugar to dredge
ORANGE BUTTER ICING:
2 oz. butter
4 oz. icing sugar
1–2 dessertspoons orange cordial

Cream fats with icing sugar and orange rind until soft and creamy. Add cornflour and beat well. Add sifted flours, a little at a time, and beat to make smooth mixture. Use icing bag with large rose nozzle to pipe mixture into rounds on greased baking trays. Cook in moderate oven (350 deg. F.—Mark 4) 12–15 minutes or till pale golden. Cool on wire rack. Sandwich together in pairs with orange butter icing, dredge with a little icing sugar.
TO PREPARE ORANGE BUTTER ICING: Cream butter and icing sugar, beat in orange cordial.

Florentines
MAKES: EIGHTEEN
2 oz. table margarine
2 oz. Demerara sugar
1 tablespoon golden syrup
2 oz. sifted self-raising flour
1½ oz. chopped glacé cherries
1½ oz. chopped walnuts and almonds
1 oz. flaked almonds
1 oz. mixed peel
5 oz. block chocolate

Grease baking sheets. Melt the table margarine, Demerara sugar and golden syrup in a saucepan over gentle heat but do not allow the mixture to become too hot. Remove from heat, stir in sifted flour, chopped glacé cherries, walnuts, almonds, flaked almonds and mixed peel. Drop in teaspoonfuls on to prepared trays, setting well apart to allow for spreading. Bake in a moderately slow oven (325 deg. F.—Mark 3) for 10–15 minutes. Remove from oven and use a knife or large plain cutter to form into clean round shapes. Leave biscuits on tray to cool for 1–2 minutes then very carefully transfer to wire rack to cool. Melt pieces of broken chocolate in bowl over a pan of hot water. Remove from heat and allow to cool slightly. When the chocolate begins to thicken, spread over the smooth side of the prepared biscuits. When chocolate is almost setting on biscuits, make wavy lines with a fork.

Ginger crisp biscuits
MAKES: SIX TO SEVEN DOZEN
8 oz. golden syrup
8 oz. margarine
6 oz. caster sugar
14 oz. plain flour
pinch of salt
3 level teaspoons ground ginger
2 level teaspoons baking powder
2 level teaspoons bicarbonate of soda
1 small beaten egg

Melt golden syrup, margarine and caster sugar together over a gentle heat. Remove from the heat. Sift flour, salt, ground ginger, baking powder and bicarbonate of soda. Gradually add to the syrup mixture alternately with the beaten egg. Beat well, turn into a bowl and leave in the refrigerator or very cool place overnight. Next day, roll out very thinly on a lightly floured board. Cut into 2½-inch rounds. Place on greased baking trays. Bake in a moderate oven (350 deg. F.—Mark 4) till cooked, about 10–15 minutes. Cool on wire tray. Store in an airtight tin.

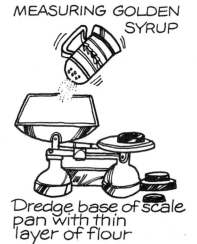
MEASURING GOLDEN SYRUP
Dredge base of scale pan with thin layer of flour

Weigh desired quantity of syrup by pouring into pan

Slide measured syrup into bowl or pan

Chef's special

Coffee house gâteau
(*Illustrated left*)

SERVES: ABOUT TEN (AS A DESSERT)

8 oz. butter or margarine
8 oz. caster sugar
4 eggs
8 oz. sifted self-raising flour
pinch of salt
2 tablespoons hot water

TOPPING AND DECORATION:

$\frac{1}{4}$ pint single cream
$\frac{1}{2}$ pint double cream
1 tablespoon caster sugar
1–2 oz. finely grated plain block chocolate
1 can (11 oz.) mandarin oranges
10 halved maraschino cherries

Grease and line a deep 10-inch sandwich tin with greaseproof paper. Use a wooden spoon to beat butter or margarine and caster sugar together until light and fluffy. Add eggs one at a time, beating really well between each addition. Use a metal spoon to fold in sifted flour and salt, add hot water to mix to a soft dropping consistency. Spread the mixture evenly over prepared tin. Cook just above centre in moderately hot oven (375 deg. F.—Mark 5) for about 45–50 minutes until well risen and pale gold. Turn out on to wire rack and leave to cool. Empty single and double creams into a bowl and whip together until thick enough to stand in peaks. Sweeten to taste. Spread sides of cake with a little of the cream then roll cake lightly in finely grated plain chocolate. Stand on a serving dish. Drain the mandarin oranges. Prick cake with a skewer and sprinkle with the mandarin juice. Spread some of the cream over top of cake. Decorate with drained mandarin oranges and halved maraschino cherries. Put remaining cream into a forcing bag fitted with a large star nozzle and pipe fancy border and centre.

VARIATIONS:

If liked a butter cream can be used instead of the fresh cream. To make this: soften 4 oz. butter in a bowl then gradually beat in 8 oz. sifted icing sugar until smooth and well blended. Add flavouring as follows:

LEMON—beat in finely grated rind of $\frac{1}{2}$ lemon and 1 tablespoon lemon juice. Decorate with peach slices instead of mandarin oranges.

ORANGE—beat in finely grated rind of $\frac{1}{2}$ orange and 1 tablespoon orange juice. Decorate with apricot halves.

CHOCOLATE—beat in 2 level tablespoons sifted cocoa dissolved in 2 tablespoons hot water. Decorate with pear halves.

COFFEE—beat in 1 level tablespoon instant coffee dissolved in 1 dessertspoon hot water. Decorate with pineapple slices.

Morning coffee party

Wholewheat gingerbread
page 135

□

Coffee house gâteau

□

Picnic slices
page 129

□

Coffee with cream
page 199

COATING CAKE SIDES

Finely grate chocolate onto greaseproof paper

Spread sides of cake with whipped cream

Roll sides of cake in chocolate until evenly coated

Chef's special

Frosted walnut layer cake

(Illustrated left)

MAKES: TWELVE SLICES
6 oz. plain flour
1 level teaspoon baking powder
6 oz. butter or margarine
5 oz. caster sugar
1 oz. soft brown sugar
pinch of salt
few drops vanilla essence
3 eggs
1 egg yolk
1 level dessertspoon instant coffee powder
1 dessertspoon hot water
3 oz. finely chopped walnuts

BUTTER ICING:
4 oz. butter
8 oz. sifted icing sugar
1 tablespoon milk

FROSTING:
8 oz. granulated sugar
$\frac{1}{8}$ pint cold water
1 stiffly whisked egg white

TO DECORATE:
walnut halves

Grease two sandwich tins, 7 inches diameter by 2 inches deep. Sift the flour and baking powder together. Cream the butter or margarine with the caster and soft brown sugar and pinch of salt until very light and fluffy. Add the vanilla essence. Whisk the eggs and yolk together lightly, then beat gradually into the creamed mixture. Dissolve the instant coffee in hot water and beat in a little at a time. Carefully fold in the sifted flour mixture and 2 oz. of the finely chopped walnuts. Turn into the prepared tins and smooth over tops with knife. Bake in centre of moderately hot oven (375 deg. F. — Mark 5) for 25–30 minutes or until well risen and golden brown. Turn out and cool on wire rack. Beat the remaining walnuts into the basic butter icing. Cut each cake in half then sandwich all the layers together with the prepared walnut butter icing. Make the frosting and pour over top and sides of cake. Decorate with walnut halves and allow to set before transferring to serving plate.

TO PREPARE BUTTER ICING: Cream the butter lightly, then beat in the sifted icing sugar until really light and fluffy. Beat in the milk.

TO PREPARE FROSTING: Place granulated sugar and water in a strong saucepan. Stir until sugar has dissolved over gentle heat then allow to boil, without stirring, to 240 deg. F. or until a teaspoon of the mixture will form a soft ball when dropped into cold water. Pour the syrup in a thin stream on to the stiffly whisked egg white. Continue whisking until mixture is thick and will coat back of spoon. Use immediately.

Afternoon tea

Afternoon tea sandwiches
page 170

☐

Viennese orange shortcakes
page 141

☐

Fruity malt loaf
page 135

☐

Frosted walnut layer cake

☐

Tea

AMERICAN FROSTING

Pour sugar syrup in thin stream onto stiffly beaten egg whites

Continue whisking till mixture is thick and coats back of spoon

Pour at once over top and sides of cake. Trim with walnut halves

Chef's special

Choux buns
(*Illustrated left*)

MAKES: SIX

2½ oz. plain flour
pinch of salt
1¾ oz. butter or margarine
¼ pint water
2 eggs

FILLING:

¼ pint double cream
3 tablespoons single cream
1–2 teaspoons caster sugar

GLACÉ ICING:

6 oz. icing sugar
1–2 tablespoons warm water
1–2 oz. melted chocolate
1 teaspoon coffee essence
little coffee-flavoured butter
    icing (see p. 143)

Sift flour and salt on to sheet of greaseproof paper. Place butter or margarine and the water into a small saucepan and bring to the boil. Remove pan from heat and add flour all at once. Beat with wooden spoon until the mixture forms a ball in the centre of the pan and leaves the sides of the pan clean. Allow mixture to cool slightly. Beat eggs together then very gradually add to the mixture, beating in each addition well but lightly until the paste is thick, smooth, glossy and holds its shape. Place the prepared paste into a forcing bag fitted with plain ½-inch pipe. Pipe six 2 inch rounds and six 1 inch rounds on a damp baking sheet. Use palette knife to flatten 1-inch rounds to form bases (see photograph left). Bake in a hot oven (400 deg. F.—Mark 6). Allow 10–15 minutes for bases and 20–25 minutes for buns, until well puffed up and golden. Remove from oven and make a small slit in the base of each bun, return to oven for 5 minutes to allow them to dry. Transfer to cooling tray to become completely cold. Whip double and single creams together until firm, fold in the caster sugar and place into a large forcing bag fitted with a plain pipe. Completely fill centre of each 2-inch bun with cream from slit in base and set each bun on a small round of choux pastry. Sift icing sugar into a bowl. Add warm water and beat with a wooden spoon until creamy consistency. Turn half the icing into another bowl and beat in melted chocolate. Add coffee essence to remainder and beat well. Use to coat tops of choux buns. Allow to set before piping a little coffee-flavoured butter icing on top of each.

After theatre supper

Egg and mushroom savoury
page 152

□

Simple salad
page 98

□

Choux buns

□

Gaelic coffee
page 183

PROFITEROLES

Make small choux buns, fill with ice cream or custard

Carefully arrange in pyramid on serving dish

Pour chocolate sauce over top

Chef's special

Christmas cake
(*Illustrated left*)
4 oz. glacé cherries
4 oz. stoned dates
4 oz. blanched almonds (optional)
3–4 oz. candied peel
1 lb. plain flour
½ level teaspoon salt
1 level teaspoon ground cinnamon
½ level teaspoon grated nutmeg
12 oz. butter or margarine
12 oz. dark brown sugar
finely grated rind of 1 lemon
6 eggs
12 oz. currants
12 oz. sultanas
12 oz. seedless raisins
2 tablespoons black treacle
2–3 tablespoons fruit juice, sherry or brandy

Grease a 9-inch cake tin and line with a doubled layer of greased greaseproof paper. Halve the glacé cherries. Chop the dates and almonds. Finely shred the candied peel. Sift the flour with the salt, cinnamon and nutmeg. Cream the butter or margarine with soft dark brown sugar and finely grated lemon rind until really light and fluffy. Add the eggs, one at a time, beating well after each addition. Fold in sifted flour mixture together with all the fruits and the nuts and black treacle, fruit juice, sherry or brandy. Turn the mixture into the prepared tin and bake on shelf below centre of a very slow oven (275 deg. F.—Mark 1) for about 5–6 hours or until cooked through. Cover with a piece of greaseproof paper after about 2½ hours. (Ovens vary considerably so test the cake before the end of cooking time.) Cool cake in tin then turn out on to cooling rack, remove paper and when cold store in airtight tin.
To almond paste and Royal Ice cake, see page 196.

Christmas tea spread

Savoury vol-au-vents
page 175

Quiche Lorraine
page 159

Fruit trifle
page 119

Auntie Flo's chocolate cake
page 133

Christmas cake

Tea or fruit drinks
page 182

CHRISTMAS CAKE DESIGNS

Pipe trellis work with a No. 3 plain piping tube

Little figures on roughed up icing make a pretty snow scene

Cut out card pattern as guide to making almond paste trees

10
Savouries and Breakfasts

Quick snacks
Breakfasts
Supper dishes
Chef's specials

Egg and mushroom savoury (*recipe overleaf*)

Quick snacks and breakfasts

Egg and mushroom savoury

SERVES: THREE TO FOUR

3 oz. butter or margarine
4 oz. washed and dried button mushrooms
8 eggs
salt
freshly ground black pepper
3 tablespoons single cream or top of the milk

TO GARNISH:

sprinkling of parsley
triangles of fried bread

Melt 1 oz. of butter or margarine in a small saucepan. Add washed and dried button mushrooms and simmer for 5 minutes till tender. Cover and keep hot. Break eggs into a bowl. Beat lightly with a fork. Season well with salt and freshly ground black pepper. Melt rest of fat in another saucepan. Pour in beaten eggs, stir with a wooden spoon over a gentle heat until mixture thickens and is lightly scrambled but is still creamy. Remove from heat and fold in cream or top of the milk. Turn immediately into a warm serving dish. Top with drained mushrooms. Garnish with a sprinkling of parsley and triangles of fried bread.

Buck rarebit

SERVES: FOUR

1 oz. butter or margarine
1 level tablespoon plain flour
5 tablespoons milk
1 level teaspoon made mustard
few drops Worcester sauce
6 oz. grated Cheddar cheese
salt and pepper
4 slices buttered toast
4 poached eggs

Melt butter or margarine in a small saucepan. Stir in flour and cook for a minute without browning. Add milk and stir well to form a smooth mixture. Add made mustard, Worcester sauce, grated Cheddar cheese and a good pinch of salt and pepper. Remove from heat and blend well. Spread on hot buttered toast, place under a hot grill until golden brown. Serve with a poached egg on top.

Bacon and potato cakes

SERVES: FOUR

6 rashers streaky bacon
1 lb. mashed potatoes
½ oz. butter or margarine
1 teaspoon finely chopped parsley
3–4 oz. plain flour
¼ level teaspoon salt
lard or cooking fat for frying

TO SERVE:

grilled tomatoes
parsley

Remove rind from bacon and discard. Grill or fry bacon until lightly brown and crisp. Chop into small pieces. Beat the mashed potatoes with butter or margarine and chopped parsley until smooth. Add the chopped bacon and gradually work in sifted flour and salt to form a firm dough. Roll out on floured board to ½-inch thickness and cut into squares. Fry in hot melted fat, turning as necessary until golden brown and cooked through. Serve hot with grilled tomatoes garnished with parsley.

TOPPINGS FOR TOAST

Fry floured roes in butter till golden. Top with lemon twist

Fry bacon and top with apple slices

Fry chipolata sausages with onion slices. Sprinkle with Worcester Sauce

Crumpets—
Pizza style

MAKES: FOUR

4 crumpets or pikelets
butter for spreading
4 oz. finely grated cheese
2 sliced tomatoes
1 can (1 oz.) anchovy fillets

TO GARNISH:

a few black olives or pickled
walnuts

Toast the crumpets or pikelets on both sides under a preheated grill and butter the tops well. Divide 2 oz. of the grated cheese between the crumpets, and spread out evenly. Add some thin slices of tomato and top with the remaining cheese. Arrange the drained anchovy fillets in a criss-cross pattern over the top. Place under a medium grill and cook till the cheese melts and turns golden brown. Garnish the tops with a piece of black olive or pickled walnut and serve at once.

Devilled kidneys

SERVES: TWO

4 lambs kidneys
1½ oz. butter
½–1 level teaspoon curry powder
a little made mustard
salt

TO SERVE:

grilled tomatoes
unbuttered toast

Remove skin from kidneys. Cut in half lengthwise with a sharp knife. Cut out core with pair of scissors (see sketch on p. 43). Melt butter in saucepan. Add kidneys and fry lightly until browned all over. Add curry powder, made mustard and salt. Cover and cook over gentle heat, stirring occasionally, for 10–15 minutes or until kidneys are tender. Serve with grilled tomatoes on unbuttered toast.

Quickie risotto

SERVES: THREE

8 oz. long grain rice
1 can (10½ oz.) condensed
    vegetable soup
½ pint water
4 oz. sliced mushrooms
2 chopped tomatoes (optional)
pinch of mixed herbs
salt and pepper
3 sliced hard-boiled eggs or
    grated cheese

Wash rice in sieve under running cold water to clean. Place vegetable soup, water and washed rice into a pan and bring slowly to boil. Add the sliced mushrooms, 2 chopped tomatoes, if liked, mixed herbs and salt and pepper to taste. Simmer for about 20 minutes, stirring as necessary till liquid is absorbed and rice is tender. Pile on serving dish and decorate round edge with sliced hard-boiled eggs or grated cheese.

TOPPINGS FOR TOAST

Grill brisling and sliced tomato on toast. Garnish with parsley

Grill cheese on top of toast. Top with tomato ketchup

Grill mushrooms. Top with sour cream. Sprinkle with chopped chives

Quick snacks

Piperade

(*Illustrated left*)

SERVES: ONE TO TWO

1 small onion
1 clove of garlic
3 rashers streaky bacon
1 tablespoon cooking oil
1 green pepper
1 red pepper
4 eggs
salt
freshly ground black pepper

Peel and chop the onion finely, crush the peeled clove of garlic, trim the rind from the bacon, cut bacon into small pieces. Heat the oil in the frying pan add the onion, garlic and bacon and fry gently until the onion is soft and transparent. Cut the tops from the green and red peppers, scoop out the seeds and discard, wash the peppers and dry thoroughly. Chop the flesh into small pieces and add to the pan. Continue to fry gently until the peppers are soft. Whisk the eggs together with the seasoning and pour into pan. Stir the ingredients lightly together with a fork then leave to settle and cook gently until the eggs have set. Serve at once.

Swedish onion casserole

SERVES: FOUR

2 large onions
1 oz. melted butter
4 sliced hard-boiled eggs
CHEESE SAUCE:
1½ oz. butter or margarine
3 level tablespoons plain flour
¾ pint milk
3–4 oz. grated cheese
salt and pepper
a little made mustard
TO GARNISH:
fried parsley (see sketches below)

Peel, slice and fry onions in melted butter, until tender and pale golden brown. Place in casserole or ovenproof dish and arrange sliced hard-boiled eggs over top. Cover with prepared cheese sauce and cook in hot oven (400 deg. F.—Mark 6) for 15–20 minutes until heated through and golden brown. TO PREPARE CHEESE SAUCE: Melt the butter or margarine in saucepan. Stir in flour and cook over gentle heat, stirring continually for 1 minute. Remove pan from heat and gradually blend in milk to form smooth sauce. Return to heat, bring to boil and simmer gently 3 minutes, stirring throughout. Stir in grated cheese and season well to taste with salt, pepper and made mustard. Garnish with fried parsley.

Buttered crab toasts

MAKES FOUR ROUNDS

2 oz. butter
8 oz. fresh crab meat
2 tablespoons fresh white bread-crumbs
1 dessertspoon chopped parsley
1 teaspoon lemon juice
freshly ground black pepper
4 rounds hot toasted bread
TO GARNISH:
lemon wedges
watercress

Melt the butter in a saucepan. Stir in the crab meat, bread-crumbs, chopped parsley, lemon juice and freshly ground black pepper to taste. Mix well then heat through gently, stirring all the time. Pile the hot mixture on to rounds of freshly made toast. Garnish top of each with a lemon wedge and a little watercress. Serve at once as a savoury snack with lettuce or as a meal starter.

FRYING PARSLEY

Wash and dry well in a cloth

Heat deep fat till slight haze appears. Draw pan from heat

Fry parsley till crisp, drain on soft kitchen paper

Supper dishes

Eggs in jackets
(*Illustrated left*)
SERVES: FOUR
4 large potatoes
1 oz. butter
salt and pepper
4 medium-sized eggs
TO SERVE:
lettuce

Scrub the potatoes and place on a lightly greased baking tray. Bake in a hot oven (400 deg. F.—Mark 6) for 1–1¼ hours till soft. Remove from the oven and cut a slice from the top of each potato. Carefully scoop out the soft potato with a teaspoon, being careful not to tear the jacket. Mash the soft potato with the butter and seasoning to taste. Divide the mixture between the jackets. Press down well leaving a hollow in the centre for an egg. Break the eggs into the hollows. Return to the oven for about 10 minutes to set. Serve with lettuce.

Scotch eggs
SERVES: THREE
3 hard-boiled eggs
½ oz. plain flour
8 oz. sausagemeat
1 small beaten egg
browned breadcrumbs for coating
deep fat for frying
TO SERVE:
buttered toast or salad

Cover hard-boiled eggs with cold water after cooking and allow to become completely cold. Remove shells and roll the eggs in flour. Divide the sausagemeat into three equal portions, roll into rounds. Place an egg on each round. Work sausagemeat evenly over each egg, making sure there are no cracks or air pockets. Coat in beaten egg and roll in browned breadcrumbs. Place in frying basket and lower into hot deep fat. Fry steadily till golden brown and sausagemeat is cooked through, about 5–10 minutes. Drain well on absorbent paper. Serve hot with buttered toast or cold with salad.

Sausage and smash
SERVES: FOUR
8 oz. haricot beans
1–1½ pints stock (made from chicken stock cube)
1 peeled chopped onion
a few bacon rinds
1 bay leaf
salt and pepper
2 oz. butter or margarine
TO SERVE:
1 lb. chipolata beef sausages
chopped parsley

Soak the haricot beans in water overnight. Drain well then place in a saucepan with the chicken stock, peeled and chopped onion, bacon rinds, bay leaf and seasoning. Bring to the boil, cover and simmer gently until the beans are tender, about 2–2½ hours. Strain off the liquid into a jug, then press beans through a sieve with a wooden spoon or pass through a liquidizer. Return the purée of beans to the pan and add the butter or margarine and, if necessary, enough of the retained liquid to make a thick purée. Re-heat and check seasoning then arrange in a serving dish. Top with fried or grilled chipolata beef sausages. Sprinkle with parsley.

JACKET BAKED POTATOES

Scrub and dry potatoes, prick with fork. Brush with oil

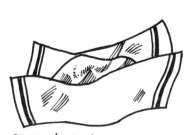

Bake in hot oven 1–1½ hours. Squeeze in cloth to test if tender

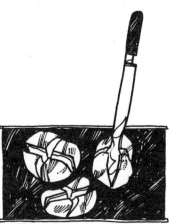

Cut cross on top. Squeeze open. Top with butter

Supper dishes

Tuna and egg tartlets

(*Illustrated left*)

MAKES: SIX

6 oz. shortcrust pastry (see p. 192)

FILLING:

2 cans (7 oz. each) tuna fish

½ pint prepared white sauce (see p. 186)

1 teaspoon anchovy essence

salt and pepper to taste

1–2 oz. grated Cheddar cheese

TO GARNISH:

3 halved hard-boiled eggs

paprika pepper

parsley sprigs

Use pastry to line six good-size individual fluted patty tins. Prick base well with a fork. Bake 'blind' in a preheated hot oven (400 deg. F.—Mark 6) for about 10 minutes or until pastry is cooked through. Remove pastry cases from patty tins. Cool slightly then transfer to baking sheet. Fill cases with prepared filling. Sprinkle with grated Cheddar cheese, return to oven 15–20 minutes until filling is heated through and cheese is golden brown. Remove from oven, place half an egg on top and sprinkle with paprika pepper. Top with parsley.

TO PREPARE FILLING: Fold flaked tuna fish into prepared white sauce together with the anchovy essence and seasoning to taste. Mix well together. Use cheese as directed above.

Quiche Lorraine

SERVES: SIX

8 oz. plain flour

pinch of salt

4 oz. butter

1 egg yolk

2–3 tablespoons water

FILLING:

1 onion

melted butter

1½ oz. cooked ham

2 eggs

cayenne pepper

½ pint milk

Sift flour and salt into bowl. Rub in butter finely. Bind together with egg yolk beaten with water. Put in a cool place 1 hour. Roll out and use to line a plain 9- or 10-inch flan ring on a baking sheet (see p. 193). Prick base lightly with a fork. Place round of greaseproof paper in flan and cover with baking beans. Bake in hot oven (400 deg. F.—Mark 6) for 10–15 minutes. Meanwhile, peel and chop onion. Cook in melted butter 5 minutes or until tender. Chop cooked ham. Beat eggs with cayenne pepper. Heat milk in saucepan, add to beaten eggs and heat gently until custard begins to thicken. Remove from heat. Reduce oven temperature to moderately hot (375 deg. F.—Mark 5). Remove paper and baking beans from flan. Cover base with cooked onion and ham. Pour over custard. Bake 30 minutes or until set.

Friday's pie

SERVES: SIX

1½ lb. smoked haddock

¾ pint milk

2 oz. butter

1 oz. flour

1 chopped hard-boiled egg

salt and pepper

1½ lb. boiled potatoes

2–3 oz. grated cheese

1 oz. chopped walnuts

Simmer smoked haddock in milk 8–10 minutes or until cooked through. Strain liquid into measuring jug. Remove skin and bones from fish and flake with a knife. Melt half the butter in saucepan, stir in flour and cook for a few seconds without browning. Remove from heat; gradually stir in strained milk. Bring to boil, simmer gently 3 minutes, stirring all the time, until smooth and thick. Add chopped hard-boiled egg, flaked fish and seasoning to taste. Slice boiled potatoes and reserve well-shaped pieces for topping. Place remainder in base of ovenproof casserole. Turn fish mixture on top of potato and overlap remaining slices on top of fish. Brush with 1 oz. melted butter and bake in a moderately hot oven (375 deg. F.—Mark 5) for 25 minutes. Sprinkle top with grated cheese and chopped walnuts. Turn up oven temperature (425 deg. F.—Mark 7). Bake 5–10 minutes or until golden brown.

GHERKIN FANS

Take firm, even-size cocktail gherkins

Slice lengthwise several times, almost to base

Spread carefully out into a fan shape

Supper dishes

Savoury pancakes with prawns

(*Illustrated left*)
MAKES: SIX TO EIGHT
4 oz. plain flour
pinch of salt
1 egg
½ pint milk
½ oz. melted butter
a little cooking oil for frying
TO SERVE:
Tomato sauce (see p. 188)
6 oz. prawns

Sift flour and salt into mixing bowl. Make well in centre. Break in whole egg and add 4 tablespoons of the milk. Stir mixture, gradually drawing in flour from sides of the bowl and adding more milk as necessary to make smooth batter. When all milk has been added stir in melted butter. Cover bowl and leave 1 hour. To make the pancakes, heat a little oil in an 8-inch frying pan until hot. Pour any surplus into a small jug. Pour 3-4 tablespoons batter into the pan to coat the base evenly. Cook until set and golden brown underneath, then carefully turn or toss pancake and cook other side. Make up pancakes with remaining batter in same way. Pour a little prepared Tomato sauce into centre of each pancake, top with 2 tablespoons peeled prawns. Carefully slip out on to a plate. Roll up and serve.

Sardine and macaroni grill

SERVES: TWO
6 oz. quick-cooking macaroni
boiling salted water
MUSHROOM SAUCE:
2 oz. butter or margarine
1 oz. plain flour
½ pint milk
4 oz. washed sliced mushrooms
salt and pepper
TOPPING:
1 tomato
1 can (4½ oz.) sardines
1 oz. grated Parmesan cheese
TO SERVE:
lettuce

Cook the macaroni in plenty of boiling salted water till tender, about 7-10 minutes. Drain well. Mix into the prepared sauce and turn into a shallow ovenproof dish. Arrange the sliced tomato with the sardines on top. Sprinkle with the grated Parmesan cheese. Place under hot grill to heat and lightly brown top. Serve with lettuce.

TO PREPARE THE SAUCE: Melt 1 oz. of the butter or margarine in a pan, mix in the flour and cook gently for 1 minute. Gradually blend in the milk to make a smooth sauce. Bring to the boil, still stirring and cook for 3 minutes. Melt remaining fat in a pan, add washed sliced mushrooms and cook gently till just tender. Mix into prepared sauce and season to taste.

Cheese and asparagus Charlotte

SERVES: THREE TO FOUR
½ oz. butter
4-5 slices buttered bread
1 can (10½ oz.) asparagus spears
4-6 oz. grated cheese
3 eggs
1 pint milk
1 level teaspoon dry mustard
salt and pepper

Lightly butter a 2½-3-pint pie dish or ovenproof dish. Trim the crusts from the buttered bread, place a layer of bread in the dish and then the drained asparagus spears. Sprinkle with half the grated cheese. Cover with remaining bread and cheese. Beat the eggs well, add the milk, dry mustard and seasoning to taste. Pour into dish and allow to stand for 15 minutes. Bake in a moderately hot oven (375 deg. F. —Mark 5) until set and golden brown, about 45-50 minutes. Serve hot.

SAVOURY FILLINGS FOR PANCAKES

Add flaked cooked haddock to cheese sauce

Add cooked mushroom slices to soured cream

Add cubes chopped ham to parsley sauce

Supper dishes

Ham and mushroom flan
(*Illustrated left*)
SERVES: FOUR TO SIX
6 oz. shortcrust pastry (see p. 192)
8 oz. piece gammon
4 oz. button mushrooms
1 tablespoon oil
1 egg
¼ pint milk
salt and pepper

Line an 8-inch fluted flan ring with pastry. Prick the base with a fork. Place a piece of grease-proof paper inside flan ring and cover with baking beans or crusts. Cook in a preheated hot oven (400 deg. F.—Mark 6) for 10 minutes. Remove from oven, remove the greaseproof paper and baking beans, return to oven for a further 5 minutes. Trim rind and cut gammon into small cubes. Wash and dry button mushrooms. Heat the oil in a frying pan, fry the ham and mushrooms together for 5 minutes. Drain off any excess fat, place ham and mushrooms in pastry case. Whisk egg, milk and seasoning together, pour into flan case and return to oven for approximately 25–30 minutes or until egg mixture has set.

Festive pie
SERVES: SIX
8 oz. shortcrust pastry (see p. 192)
8 oz. diced cooked chicken or ham
3–4 tablespoons thick white sauce
2–3 tablespoons finely grated Cheddar cheese
salt
freshly ground black pepper
1 large thinly sliced tomato
1 small chopped green pepper
a little milk to glaze

Make up the pastry and roll out half, line a 7½-inch pie plate. Place half the diced chicken or ham on top. Cover with sauce and sprinkle with a little of the finely grated cheese. Season well. Cover with thin slices of tomato. Blanch the chopped green pepper in boiling water for 1 minute, then drain well and scatter over the tomato. Cover with remaining meat and cheese, add seasoning. Roll out remaining pastry for lid. Damp pastry edges and place lid into position. Knock up and flute edges with the back of a knife. Cut slit in centre of pie for steam to escape during cooking. Brush with milk. Bake on shelf, above centre of a hot oven (400 deg. F.—Mark 6) for about 40 minutes until pastry is golden brown and cooked.

Crisp chicken rolls
SERVES: TWO
4 crisp dinner rolls
a little melted butter
a little paprika pepper
FILLING:
1 can (10½ oz.) condensed cream of mushroom soup
2 tablespoons cream or top of the milk
4–5 oz. diced cooked chicken

Cut a lid from each roll with a sharp knife then scoop out most of the inner crumb with a tea-spoon. Brush inside of rolls with melted butter and put into hot oven until heated through, about 5 minutes. Spoon a little filling into the centre of each roll, then sprinkle with paprika pepper. Serve hot.
TO PREPARE FILLING: Blend cream of mushroom soup with cream or top of the milk and stir in diced chicken. Cook in pan over gentle heat 3–4 minutes.

BACON ROLLS

Trim rind from rashers with scissors or knife

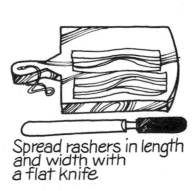

Spread rashers in length and width with a flat knife

Cut in half, roll up. Thread on skewers before cooking

Chef's special

Cheese soufflé
(*Illustrated left*)

SERVES: FOUR

a little butter for greasing
½ pint milk
1 small peeled onion
2–3 cloves
1 bay leaf
2 oz. butter
scant 1 oz. flour
5 egg yolks
4 oz. finely grated Cheddar
  cheese
salt
freshly ground black pepper
½ teaspoon made mustard
6 egg whites

Preparations are all important when making a soufflé. Choose a 2½-pint soufflé dish (7½ inches in diameter) for the above quantity of mixture. Butter dish lightly. Preheat oven to hot (400 deg. F.—Mark 6). See shelf is set in correct position, the centre shelf, and place a baking sheet on the shelf to get hot so that when the soufflé dish is set on this it will start cooking at once. Place the milk in a saucepan with the onion which has been studded with cloves. Add bay leaf and place over a gentle heat for 3–4 minutes until almost boiling. Cover with lid and draw away from heat. Allow to infuse for 15–20 minutes then strain milk into a bowl or jug to use in the sauce. Melt 2 oz. butter in another pan, stir in flour, remove from heat and stir in strained milk. Beat well to form a thick smooth sauce. Return to heat, allow to come to boil then remove from heat. Do not overcook at this stage or the soufflé will not rise properly. Allow the sauce to cool a little then gradually beat in egg yolks. Stir in finely grated Cheddar cheese, salt, freshly ground black pepper and made mustard. Mixture can be prepared to this stage in advance.

Place the egg whites in a clean, dry bowl. Whisk with a spiral or balloon wire whisk until creamy and standing up in peaks. Turn half the whisked whites into the basic mixture in a bowl. Turn the bowl with one hand and fold in the whites with a metal spoon, lifting and folding throughout. Add remaining whites and repeat the folding-in process which should result in a spongy, frothy mass. Have the prepared soufflé dish to hand, pour in mixture which will come about three-quarters up sides of dish. Mark a deep circle in soufflé mixture 1 inch or so from the edge of the dish with a knife. Centre section of the soufflé will rise to give a cottage loaf effect. Place soufflé in preheated oven on the hot baking sheet. Cook for about 35 minutes, until well risen and golden brown. Remove carefully from oven on baking sheet and transfer to a slightly warmed plate. Serve immediately.

Cheese soufflé

□

Gina's salad
page 99

or Green salad
page 98

□

Hot apricot slices
page 113

Suggested wine for main course:
Barbera

VARIATIONS
ON SOUFFLÉ

In place of cheese...

Add 6 oz chopped cooked mushrooms to béchamel sauce

Add 3-4 tablespoons cooked flaked haddock to béchamel sauce

Add 3oz melted chocolate and 2oz sugar to plain sauce

Chef's special

Stuffed aubergines
(*Illustrated left*)

SERVES: TWO

2 aubergines (approximately 6 oz. each)
3 oz. fresh white breadcrumbs
1 small onion
4 oz. button mushrooms
1 teaspoon mixed herbs
salt and pepper
1 beaten egg
1 oz. melted butter
½ pint prepared Tomato sauce (see p. 188)

TO GARNISH:
sprigs of parsley

Wash aubergines, remove stalks and cut into halves lengthwise. Scoop out seeds and discard, then remove some of the flesh and chop finely. Place breadcrumbs in a bowl. Peel and coarsely grate onion, add to breadcrumbs with chopped aubergines, washed and finely chopped button mushrooms, mixed herbs and seasoning. Bind together with beaten egg and divide evenly between 4 aubergine halves. Smooth top with knife and brush with melted butter. Set prepared aubergines in prepared Tomato sauce in base of ovenproof dish. Cover and cook in a moderate oven (350 deg. F.—Mark 4) for 40–45 minutes then remove cover and continue to cook for further 20–25 minutes or until lightly browned on top. Garnish with sprigs of parsley.

Alternative meat filling

SERVES: TWO

2 aubergines
2 tablespoons oil
1 small peeled sliced onion
1 small finely crushed clove of garlic
1 small chopped green pepper
8 oz. minced beef
salt and pepper
a good pinch of marjoram
1 oz. breadcrumbs
2 oz. grated cheese
½ pint prepared Tomato sauce (see p. 188)

Prepare the aubergines as in recipe on left. Heat oil in pan, add peeled and sliced onion, finely crushed clove of garlic and chopped green pepper and cook till just tender. Add minced beef and cook till brown all over. Mix in seasoning to taste, marjoram, chopped aubergine flesh and crumbs. Divide mixture between 4 aubergine halves, sprinkle with cheese. Set aubergines in prepared Tomato sauce in base of casserole. Cover and cook in a moderate oven (350 deg. F.—Mark 4) for 30 minutes then remove cover and continue cooking for a further 15 minutes or until lightly brown on top.

Stuffed aubergines
Potato croquettes
page 90

□

Caramel custard
page 115

Suggested wine for main course:
Bardolino

STUFFED GREEN PEPPERS

Cut tops off peppers and scoop out seeds

Parboil in salted boiling water 5 minutes. Drain well

Fill with stuffing. Cover with foil. Bake in hot oven 45 minutes

11
Sandwiches

Open sandwiches
Teatime fillings
Fried sandwiches

Danish open sandwiches (*recipe overleaf*)

Open sandwiches · fillings

Danish open sandwiches

1 thin slice buttered rye bread for each sandwich

CHICKEN TOPPING:

few lettuce leaves
1 cooked chicken joint
1 rasher grilled streaky bacon
few slices cucumber
small tomato wedge
sprig of parsley

Arrange lettuce leaves on a slice of buttered rye bread, top with chicken joint and grilled streaky bacon. Garnish with twists of sliced cucumber, tomato wedge and parsley.

SALAMI TOPPING:

3 slices salami sausage
few lettuce leaves
few rings peeled raw onion
sprigs of parsley

Arrange 2 slices salami on a slice of buttered rye bread. Make a cut from centre of remaining slice to outer edge. Curl the two ends round till they meet to make a neatly shaped cone. Place in middle of sandwich. Garnish centre of cone with lettuce and onion rings. Decorate with parsley.

EGG TOPPING:

few lettuce leaves
6 slices hard-boiled egg
1 tablespoon home-made or bought mayonnaise
1 tablespoon Danish mock caviar
small tomato wedge
sprig of parsley

Arrange the lettuce on slice of buttered rye bread. Lay sliced hard-boiled egg over, lapped in two neat rows. Pipe or spoon mayonnaise down the centre. Top with 'caviar'. Garnish with tomato wedge and parsley.

PORK LUNCHEON MEAT TOPPING:

1 large slice pork luncheon meat
1 tablespoon mayonnaise
1 thick slice orange
1 large cooked prune
sprig of parsley
lettuce leaf

Arrange pork luncheon meat on slice of buttered rye bread. Tuck one end under and make a neat fold in centre. Spoon mayonnaise at one end behind the fold. Make cut from centre of orange slice to outer edge. Arrange on sandwich. Top with prune and garnish with parsley and lettuce leaf.

Afternoon tea sandwiches

FILLINGS FOR WHITE BREAD AND BUTTER:

1. Mix 2 oz. shrimps or prawns with 1 tablespoon mayonnaise. Add salt and pepper to taste and stir in 1 tablespoon grated cucumber or cucumber slices. Makes two rounds.

2. Blend 1 teaspoon ready-made mustard into 1 oz. butter and use to spread bread slices. Cover with thin slices of cooked ham. Makes three rounds.

3. Blend 2 oz. cream cheese with ½ oz. chopped blanched almonds and a little finely grated orange rind. Makes one round.

FILLINGS FOR BROWN BREAD AND BUTTER:

1. Lay thin slices of smoked salmon on bread and butter and sprinkle with lemon juice and freshly ground black pepper. Sandwich with second slice of bread and butter. 4 oz. smoked salmon makes three to four rounds.

2. Finely chop 1 hard-boiled egg and blend with 1–2 dessertspoons mayonnaise and 1 teaspoon finely chopped parsley. Makes two rounds.

3. Lay slices of cooked chicken on bread and butter and crumble crisply fried bacon over the top. Makes one round.

ASPARAGUS ROLLS

Trim crusts from thin slices buttered bread

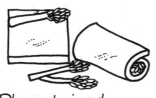

Place drained asparagus tip on bread. Roll up firmly

Pack in slightly damp cloth for 1 hour before serving

Fried Sandwiches

All time favourite

Blend together 2–3 oz. minced or finely chopped luncheon meat with 1 skinned finely chopped tomato. Season with salt and pepper. Lightly spread two buttered slices bread with mustard and sandwich together with filling. Press firmly at edges. Dip in beaten egg (3–4 tablespoons milk may be added to egg if several rounds are being made), fry the sandwich in 4–5 tablespoons hot fat, on both sides, until golden brown in frying pan. Cut in half or into quarters to serve. Garnish with a sprig of parsley. Makes one round.

Bacon bounty

Mix 2–3 rashers chopped grilled bacon with 1 mashed banana. Spread between two buttered bread slices as filling and proceed for frying as above. Makes one round.

Sailor Sam special

Drain oil from can ($4\frac{1}{2}$ oz.) of sardines. Mash sardines and moisten with a little tomato ketchup and a pinch of dried basil or mixed herbs. Proceed as before for frying. Makes one round.

Onion savoury

Peel and slice onion into very thin rings. Cook in 1 oz. melted butter until tender. Remove from pan and add to 2–3 oz. coarsely grated cheese in a bowl and use as filling. Fry as before. Makes one round.

Yorkshire treat

Spread buttered bread slices with a little made mustard and pieces of cooked ham (about 1 oz.). Blend 2 oz. grated cheese to spreading consistency with 2 teaspoons Yorkshire Relish or Worcester sauce and spread on top. Sandwich together. Dip in egg and fry as before. Makes one round.

Pub special

Spread bread slices with paté ($2\frac{1}{4}$ oz. can is ideal for this). Top with pickle and fry as before. Makes one round.

Children's choice

Spread bread with 1 teaspoonful peanut butter, top with 1 oz. sultanas. Sandwich together, fry as before. Makes one round.

Family favourite

Spread bread slices with 1 tablespoon peanut butter, then with 1 dessertspoon honey. Sandwich together. Proceed as before for frying. Makes one round.

Cheese savoury

Spread bread slices thinly with meat or vegetable extract, then sprinkle with 2 oz. grated Cheddar cheese. Sandwich together. Proceed as before for frying. Makes one round.

GARLIC BREAD

Slice French loaf at $\frac{1}{2}$–1 inch intervals without cutting right through

Blend 3ozs butter with crushed clove of garlic. Spread in incisions

Wrap in kitchen foil. Heat in hot oven 10–15 minutes.

12 Party Snacks

Menus

Devils on horseback (*recipe overleaf*)

Party snacks

Devils on horseback

MAKES: SEVEN

7 large prunes
½ can (1 oz.) drained anchovy fillets
7 blanched almonds
½ rasher de-rinded streaky bacon for each prune

TO SERVE:

small savoury biscuits

Pour boiling water over prunes and leave on one side for 30 minutes. Drain off water and carefully stone prunes. Wrap a drained anchovy fillet round each blanched almond. Place one in each stoned prune. Flatten each half rasher of bacon on a board and wrap round a stuffed prune. Place prunes on a baking sheet and bake on shelf above centre of a hot oven (400 deg. F.—Mark 6) for 8–10 minutes. Pierce each prune with a decorative cocktail stick, transfer to a plate. Serve with small savoury biscuits.

Cheese aigrettes

MAKES: ABOUT FORTY

4 oz. plain flour
pinch of salt
pinch of cayenne pepper
2 oz. butter
½ pint water
2 beaten eggs
3 oz. grated Parmesan cheese
deep fat for frying

Sift flour, salt and cayenne pepper together, leave in a warm place. Place the butter and water together in a pan to melt. When just on to boiling point remove from the heat and beat in sifted flour mixture till smooth and leaving sides of pan. Cool slightly, then add the beaten eggs a little at a time to form a smooth mixture, stir in Parmesan cheese. Fry teaspoonfuls of mixture in deep hot fat for about 8–10 minutes till crisp. Do not cook too quickly or the outsides of the aigrettes will be brown before the inside is cooked. Drain well. Serve hot.

Pork puffs

MAKES: ABOUT FOURTEEN

1 packet (13½ oz.) frozen puff pastry
a little flour
1 can (12 oz.) chopped ham and pork loaf
1 teaspoon made mustard
1 beaten egg
a little fat for greasing

Thaw the pastry at room temperature according to the packet directions for about 1 hour. Roll out on to a lightly floured board very thinly. Cut the meat loaf into even-sized fingers about ½ inch thick. Cut pastry into pieces approximately 3 by 3½ inches and place a finger of ham and pork on each, spread with a little made mustard. Brush pastry edges with beaten egg. Roll up, seal edges. Place rolls on lightly greased baking sheet. Brush each roll with beaten egg and bake just above centre of hot oven (425 deg. F.—Mark 7) for about 30 minutes or until well risen and golden brown. Serve hot or cold.

SAUSAGE ROLLS

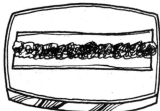

Lay rolls of sausage meat down centre of pastry strips

Damp edges of pastry, fold down edges and press down well

Knock up edges, cut into equal lengths. Mark with knife

Savoury vol-au-vents

MAKES: APPROXIMATELY EIGHT

8 oz. prepared or bought puff
    pastry
little beaten egg

TO GARNISH:
sprigs of parsley

FILLING:
3 oz. button mushrooms
1 oz. melted butter
salt and pepper
3 oz. ham (in thick slices)
½ pint Plain white sauce (see p. 186)

TO PREPARE THE CASES: Roll out pastry ⅛ inch thick on a lightly floured board. Use a 4-inch fluted pastry cutter to cut into rounds. Using a smaller cutter (2½ inches) mark each round, cutting halfway through pastry. Place on a damp baking sheet. Leave in a cool place for 30 minutes. Brush tops with beaten egg. Bake towards top of very hot oven (450 deg. F.—Mark 8) for about 10–15 minutes, until pastry is well risen and golden brown. Transfer vol-au-vents to a wire rack. Remove the lids from the cases. Fill cooled cases with the prepared filling. Arrange on plate, garnish with parsley. If liked the vol-au-vents can be heated through before serving.

TO PREPARE FILLING: Wash and drain the button mushrooms. Simmer in melted butter for 8 minutes till tender. Season to taste, drain and allow to cool. Cut ham into neat cubes. Fold mushrooms and ham into sauce. Check the seasoning.

Mini rissoles

MAKES: ABOUT THIRTY-SIX

8 oz. minced veal
8 oz. minced pork
1 small chopped onion
1 dessertspoon plain flour
salt and pepper
1 small beaten egg
a little hot butter
fat for frying

TO GARNISH:
small pieces of beetroot

Mix minced veal and pork together with chopped onion, flour and seasoning. Bind the mixture with beaten egg. Use a teaspoon dipped in hot butter to form mixture into small balls. Fry gently in hot shallow fat, turning until brown and cooked through. Drain, top each rissole with a small piece of beetroot secured with a cocktail stick. Serve hot.

Cheese straws

MAKES: ABOUT SEVENTY-TWO

8 oz. plain flour
½ level teaspoon each salt and
    dry mustard
pinch of cayenne pepper
4 oz. margarine
4 oz. finely grated Cheddar cheese
cold water to mix

Sift flour with salt, dry mustard and cayenne pepper into a bowl. Rub in margarine lightly until mixture resembles fine breadcrumbs. Mix in finely grated Cheddar cheese. Bind together with sufficient cold water to make a stiff dough. Roll out the pastry ⅛ inch thick on lightly floured board, cut into 4-inch strips (see sketches below), then cut into straws. Lay on a baking tray flat or twisted. Also stamp out six to eight rings using two round cutters (2 inch and 1¾ inch), place on baking tray. Bake towards top in hot oven (400 deg. F.—Mark 6) about 10 minutes or until golden brown. Cool on a wire tray. To serve, arrange the straws in small bundles through the rings.

CUTTING CHEESE STRAWS

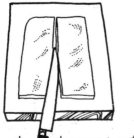

Roll out cheese pastry 10 inches wide, 6 inches long. Cut in half with floured knife

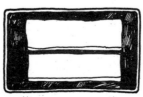

Transfer to baking sheet

Before baking, use floured knife to cut straws every ¼ inch

Party snacks

Party dip
(*Illustrated left*)

1 Dutch Edam cheese

FILLING:

2 lb. curd cheese
4 tablespoons mayonnaise
2 teaspoons horseradish relish
1 tablespoon finely chopped
   onion
3 to 4 tablespoons chopped
   capers
salt
paprika pepper

TO SERVE:

potato crisps
savoury biscuits
raw carrots

Remove slice from top of Dutch Edam cheese. Remove most of cheese from inside with a vegetable scoop, making small balls which can be served separately. Hollow out remaining cheese with a teaspoon (this can be grated and used for other dishes). Pile the prepared filling into the cheese shell, place in refrigerator to chill for about 30 minutes. Serve with small dishes of potato crisps, savoury biscuits and raw carrots for dunking.

TO PREPARE FILLING: Blend curd cheese, mayonnaise and horseradish relish together. Stir in chopped onion and capers. Season with salt and paprika pepper.

Cream cheese and watercress dip

1 bunch watercress
6 spring onions
8 oz. cream cheese
2–3 tablespoons tomato juice
salt and pepper
paprika pepper
a few drops of Tabasco or
   Worcester sauce

TO SERVE:

even-sized pieces of cucumber
raw carrots
radishes
celery sticks

Trim and discard stalks from watercress, rinse, drain and chop leaves finely. Remove roots and any discoloured tops from spring onions. Chop finely. Turn cream cheese into a bowl and blend to a smooth mixture with tomato juice. Add chopped watercress and spring onions. Season with salt, pepper and paprika pepper. Add a few drops of Tabasco or Worcester sauce. Turn into a bowl in centre of large dish surrounded by pieces of raw vegetables on cocktail sticks.

Swiss fondue

SERVES: FOUR TO SIX

1 clove of garlic
2 oz. butter
2 oz. peeled shallots
2 oz. button mushrooms
½ bottle dry white wine
12 oz. Swiss Emmenthal cheese
12 oz. Gruyère cheese
2 oz. Sbrinz or Appenzel cheese
few drops Maggi seasoning
¼ level teaspoon each dry mustard,
   pepper, paprika pepper,
   ground nutmeg
2 tablespoons sherry
3 level teaspoons cornflour

TO SERVE:

1 loaf French bread

Rub peeled clove of garlic round sides of a fondue pan. Melt the butter in it then add the peeled shallots and button mushrooms. Cook for 5–10 minutes till tender. Stir in the dry white wine and heat till warm (but do not bring to the boil). Coarsely grate cheeses, add to mixture, stirring continuously. When cheeses are melted stir in Maggi seasoning, dry mustard, pepper, paprika pepper, ground nutmeg, and sherry blended with cornflour. Bring almost to boil then simmer 15 minutes, stirring constantly in form of a figure eight. Stand fondue on regulated spirit stove so that it can be kept simmering. Guests eat fondue straight from pan, by dipping in pieces of bread on a fondue fork.

DUNKS FOR DIPS

Freshly cooked frozen crispy cod fries. Spike with cocktail sticks

Topped and tailed radishes

Cocktail size cooked sausages

Party menus

Dips and dunks

Cream cheese and watercress dip
page 177

Party dip
page 177

Suggested dunks
page 177—sketches

Cheese straws
page 175

Devils on horseback
page 174

Cheese aigrettes
page 174

Suggested wine:
Lutomer Riesling

Spanish party

Gazpacho
page 17

□

Chicken Andalusia
page 75

Green salad
page 98

□

Rich vanilla ice cream
page 117

Rich chocolate sauce
page 187

Suggested wine for main course:
Spanish dry white wine

Dinner party—1

Grilled grapefruit
page 9

□

New England chicken casserole
page 72

Potato croquettes
page 90

Green salad
page 98

□

Meringues Chantilly
page 125

Suggested wine:
Anjou Rosé

Dinner party—2

Liver pâté
page 9

□

Coq au vin
page 83

New potatoes

Courgettes

□

Lemon sorbet
page 119

Suggested wine:
Valpolicella

Informal supper party

Moussaka
page 51

Simple or Green salad
page 98

□

Lemon soufflé pie
page 115

Suggested wine for main course:
Pouilly Fuissé

Supper on the terrace

Italian tomato cocktail
page 182

□

Roast chicken with celery stuffing
page 72

Green salad
page 98

□

Lemon meringue pie
page 123

Suggested wine:
St. Emilion

Wedding anniversary

Melon with prawn cocktail
page 8

□

Cold roast turkey with peanut stuffing
pages 79, 190

Baked forehock with pineapple and sweetcorn
page 41

Cranberry or Cumberland sauce

New potatoes

Various salads
pages 98-103

□

Fruit trifle
page 119

Suggested wine:

Sparkling White Burgundy-Kriter

Wedding buffet—1

Various sandwiches
pages 170-1

Savoury vol-au-vents
page 175

Mini rissoles
page 175

Pork puffs
page 174

Liver pâté
page 9

Quiche Lorraine
page 159

Meringues Chantilly
page 125

Jap cakes
page 128

Coffee house gâteau
page 143

Suggested wine:

Italian sparkling wine Asti Gancia

Wedding buffet—2

Stuffed eggs
page 8

Savoury vol-au-vents
page 175

Cold turkey and ham
page 79

Various salads
page 98-103

Coffee house gâteau
page 143

Wedding cake

Suggested wine:

French sparkling white wine Vouvray

Scandinavian supper

Danish open sandwiches
page 170

⊔

Danish hazelnut dessert
page 121

Suggested drink:

Danish Lager

Coffee morning

Fruity malt loaf
page 135

Picnic slices
page 129

Wholewheat gingerbread
page 135

Coffee with milk or cream
page 198

Picnic party

Cream of cucumber soup
page 17

□

Chicken pâté
page 73
or Glazed meat loaf
page 61

French bread and butter

Simple salad
page 98

Selection of cheeses

□

Brandied fruit pie
page 107
or
Summer fruit salad and cream
page 111

Suggested wine:

Niersteiner Domtal

Afternoon tea

Afternoon tea sandwiches
page 170

Devonshire splits
page 139

Frangipan tartlets
page 128

Auntie Flo's chocolate cake
page 133

Tea with milk or lemon

13
Drinks

Iced citrus, Mocha special
and Italian tomato cocktail (*recipes overleaf*)

Cold drinks

Iced citrus

SERVES: TWO

2 large oranges
1 lemon
2 tablespoons sugar
½ pint boiling water
ice cubes

Wash the oranges and lemon and peel the rind thinly, being careful not to remove any of the white pith. Squeeze the juice from the fruit. Place rind in heatproof bowl, together with sugar and juice and pour ½ pint boiling water over. Leave to stand until cool then strain into glasses and add a few ice cubes.

Mocha special

SERVES: TWO

1 level teaspoon powdered instant coffee
1 teaspoon powdered drinking chocolate
1 dessertspoon boiling water
½ pint chilled milk
sugar to taste
a few small chips of ice

Blend the instant coffee and drinking chocolate powders together with boiling water, then whisk in chilled milk. Add sugar to taste. Pour into glasses, add a little chipped ice to each before serving.

Italian tomato cocktail

SERVES: THREE TO FOUR

1 can (15 oz.) tomato juice
1 lemon
freshly ground black pepper
a few ice cubes

Chill the tomato juice. Cut lemon in half, reserve 3–4 thin slices for garnish. Squeeze juice from rest of the lemon, then blend with the tomato juice and season well with black pepper. Pour cocktail into glasses, add ice cubes and garnish with the lemon slices.

Chocolate topknot

SERVES: TWO

1 well-heaped dessertspoon powdered drinking chocolate
2 teaspoons boiling water
½ pint chilled milk
2–3 teaspoons syrup from preserved ginger
a little whipped double cream

TO DECORATE:

1 piece chopped preserved ginger

Blend the drinking chocolate with the boiling water. Whisk in the chilled milk and ginger syrup. Pour into stemmed glasses. Top with whipped double cream and decorate with chopped preserved ginger.

Anniversary cup

SERVES: TWELVE

2 oranges
½ teacup chipped ice or ice cubes
2 bottles Rosé wine
¼ pint brandy
½ siphon soda water

TO DECORATE:

1 sliced lemon
sprigs of fresh mint

Squeeze juice from the oranges and pour through a strainer into punch bowl over the chipped ice. Add Rosé wine and brandy and mix well together. Top up with soda water and decorate with slices of lemon and sprigs of fresh mint just before serving.

Zip along

SERVES: TWELVE

2–3 dessertspoons sugar
strained juice of 3 oranges
1 bottle vintage cider
soda water

Dissolve the sugar in strained orange juice in punch bowl. Stir in vintage cider and an equal quantity of soda water just before serving.

FROSTING GLASSES

Invert glass rim in ¼ inch lemon juice or water

Shake, then dip in castor sugar

TRIMMING A PUNCH BOWL

Fix sprigs holly on to rim of bowl with clear sticky tape

Hot drinks

Red wine punch

SERVES: TEN TO TWELVE

6–8 cloves
1 orange
1 lemon
2 bottles Rioja
5–6 tablespoons rum
1–2 heaped tablespoons Demerara
   sugar
a few cinnamon sticks

Press cloves into whole orange and lemon. Place them in a moderate oven (350 deg. F.—Mark 4) for 30 minutes. Pour the red wine into a large bowl over pan of hot water. Keep over heat till wine is thoroughly heated through. Add rum and Demerara sugar. Stir for a few minutes. Remove orange and lemon from the oven and float them in the punch, together with cinnamon sticks. Serve hot in thick glasses.

Parting punch

SERVES: EIGHT

1 bottle dry white Bordeaux wine
2 liqueur glasses brandy
juice of 1 lemon
3 tablespoons honey

Mix all ingredients well together and heat without boiling. Serve in strong glasses.

Rum punch

SERVES: TWELVE

1 lemon
2 oz. loaf sugar
1 level teaspoon cinnamon
½ pint each rum and brandy
1 glass sherry (2 fluid oz.)
1–1½ pints boiling water
sugar to taste

Wash and dry the lemon, then rub cubes of sugar all over rind to remove the zest. Squeeze juice from lemon and strain over sugar. Add cinnamon and mix well then pour into punch bowl. Add rum, brandy, sherry and boiling water. Sweeten to taste, leave in warm place for 20 minutes before serving.

Lemon and honey drink

SERVES: TWO

1 tablespoon clear honey
1 tablespoon Demerara sugar
½ pint hot water
2 lemons

Dissolve the honey and Demerara sugar in a little of the hot water. Add juice of 1½ lemons. Add more hot water to taste. Pour into small mugs or cups and top with thin slices cut from remaining lemon half. Serve immediately.

Egg nog

SERVES: TWO

½ pint milk
1 tablespoon sugar
1 egg
1 tablespoon brandy (optional)

Heat the milk with the sugar. Separate the egg and whisk up the white until frothy. Using same whisk, beat the egg yolk into the heated milk. Stir in brandy if using, and egg white. Serve immediately.

Gaelic coffee

SERVES: ONE

2 lumps sugar
3 tablespoons Irish whiskey
hot black coffee
lightly whipped cream

Warm a large glass for each guest. Place sugar in glass. Pour in whiskey. Add piping hot coffee and stir. Dip a teaspoon in the coffee and hold it just above liquid level. Pour in the cream over the spoon so that it floats on top. The true flavour is obtained by drinking hot coffee and whisky through the cream.

GAELIC COFFEE

Put sugar and measure Irish Whiskey into strong warmed wine glass

Add piping hot coffee and stir

Pour cream over back of teaspoon to float on top

14

Sauces

Savoury sauces
Sweet sauces
Traditional sauces
Salad dressings

Plain white sauce (*recipe overleaf*)

Savoury sauces

Plain white sauce

1 oz. butter or margarine
1 oz. plain flour
½ pint milk
salt and pepper

Melt butter or margarine in small pan, but do not allow it to brown. Remove from heat, stir in flour. Stir over gentle heat for about 1 minute until the mixture bubbles and looks like honeycomb. Remove pan from the heat and gradually blend in the milk, a little at a time, beating in each addition to prevent any lumps forming and to keep the sauce as smooth as possible. Season well to taste. Return pan to gentle heat, bring to boil, simmer gently, stirring all the time for 3 minutes to form smooth and glossy sauce, thick enough to coat the back of a spoon.

Béchamel sauce

½ pint milk
1 small peeled onion
6 cloves
1 small peeled carrot
4 peppercorns
1 bay leaf
1 oz. butter or margarine
1 oz. plain flour
salt and pepper

Place the milk in a small pan. Stud the peeled onion with the cloves. Add the onion, peeled carrot, peppercorns and bay leaf to the pan. Bring slowly to the boil, remove from the heat, cover and leave in a warm place to infuse. Strain milk into a jug. Melt the butter or margarine in a pan, mix in the flour, stir over gentle heat 1 minute. Blend in the flavoured milk, stirring to make a smooth sauce. Bring to boil, then simmer and cook 3 minutes, stirring. Season to taste. Use as a basis for rich savoury sauces.

Cheese sauce

½ pint Plain white sauce (see recipe left)
½ level teaspoon made mustard
2 oz. finely grated Parmesan cheese or 4 oz. finely grated strong Cheddar cheese

To cooked Plain white sauce add made mustard and finely grated Parmesan or Cheddar cheese. Heat without boiling until the cheese has melted. Use to coat poached eggs as a supper dish. For coating macaroni cheese make up sauce with an extra ¼ pint milk or liquid strained from the cooked macaroni.

Egg sauce

½ pint Plain white sauce (see recipe left)
2 chopped hard-boiled eggs
little cayenne pepper

To the prepared Plain white sauce add chopped hard-boiled eggs and cayenne pepper to taste. Heat through. Serve with ham or bacon dishes.

Parsley sauce

½ pint hot Plain white sauce (see recipe left)
1–2 tablespoons finely chopped parsley

To the hot prepared Plain white sauce add the finely chopped parsley. Serve with poached or fried fish or pour over broad beans.

Mushroom sauce

½ pint Béchamel sauce (see recipe left)
1 oz. butter
4 oz. sliced button mushrooms
1 tablespoon top of the milk or cream

Make up the Béchamel sauce. Melt butter in a separate pan and cook the sliced button mushrooms till tender, about 5 minutes. Mix into the Béchamel sauce and heat gently for a few minutes. Just before serving add the top of the milk or cream.

WHITE SAUCE

Melt butter, sprinkle in flour. Stir one minute over gentle heat

Remove from heat, gradually blend in milk

Bring to boil, simmer 3 minutes, stirring throughout. Season

Sweet sauces

Vanilla sauce

½ oz. cornflour
½ pint milk
1 dessertspoon sugar
a few drops vanilla essence

Blend the cornflour to a smooth paste with a tablespoon milk. Heat the remaining milk and when hot but not boiling, stir into the blended cornflour. Return sauce to the pan, and bring to the boil, cook for 3 minutes, stirring all the time. Remove from the heat and add the sugar and vanilla essence. Serve with steamed puddings or stewed fruit.

Rich custard sauce

1 pint milk
2 teaspoons cornflour
3 tablespoons sugar
pinch of salt
4 beaten eggs
½ teaspoon vanilla essence

Heat milk to boiling point and set aside. Mix the cornflour, sugar and salt together in a large bowl. Gradually stir in beaten eggs, then pour in the milk. Strain into a double boiler and stir over a gentle heat until the custard thickens. Allow to cool then stir in the vanilla essence.

Rich chocolate sauce

4 oz. plain block chocolate
1 oz. butter or margarine
5 tablespoons milk
2 teaspoons rum (optional)

Break the plain chocolate into small pieces. Place in a small saucepan with the butter or margarine and milk, and place over a very gentle heat. Stir continuously till the chocolate has completely melted, then if liked add rum.

Lemon sauce

½ oz. cornflour
finely grated rind of 1 lemon
juice of 1 lemon made up to ½
    pint with water
1 oz. butter
1–2 oz. sugar

Blend cornflour and lemon rind to a smooth paste with a little of the lemon liquid. Heat the remaining liquid with the butter and when hot, but not boiling, mix into the blended cornflour. Return to the pan, bring to the boil, cook for 3 minutes stirring all the time. Remove from heat and mix in sugar to taste. Serve the sauce cold or hot with vanilla ice cream or fruit puddings.

Orange brandy sauce

2 level tablespoons cornflour
1 pint milk
finely grated rind of 1 orange
2–3 oz. caster sugar
½ oz. butter
1–2 tablespoons brandy

Blend the cornflour with a little of the milk. Bring the remainder of milk to the boil with grated orange rind, then pour on to the cornflour paste, stirring well. Return to the saucepan and boil for 3–4 minutes, stirring continuously. Add caster sugar, butter and brandy then stir till well blended. Serve with Christmas pudding or Granny's raisin pudding.

Natillas sauce

pinch of salt
2 oz. caster sugar
1 egg
2 egg yolks
1 rounded teaspoon cornflour
½ teaspoon vanilla essence
1 pint single cream

Blend the salt, caster sugar, egg, egg yolks, cornflour and vanilla essence well together in a bowl. Heat the cream, but do not boil, and mix into the blended mixture. Place the bowl over a pan of gently boiling water and cook, stirring all the time, until the mixture thickens and coats the back of the spoon. Chill in a cool place or refrigerator. Serve with fresh fruit salads or any soft fruit.

SYRUP SAUCE

Blend
1 Tablespoon cornflour
with juice of 1 lemon

Stir in just under
½ pint water and
4 tablespoons golden syrup

Stir over gentle heat
5–8 minutes till sauce
boils and thickens

Traditional sauces

Bread sauce

¾ pint milk
1 peeled onion studded with 6 cloves
1 bay leaf
3 oz. fresh white breadcrumbs
1 oz. butter
salt and pepper

Pour milk into a saucepan. Add prepared onion and bay leaf and heat gently to simmering point. Remove from the heat, cover and leave for 1–2 hours in a warm place to infuse. Strain the milk and return to the saucepan. Add breadcrumbs together with butter. Season to taste and heat slowly for about 15 minutes till sauce becomes thick and creamy. Add more milk if required. Serve with roast chicken, turkey, fried or grilled sausages.

Apple sauce

1 lb. cooking apples
3–4 tablespoons water
½ oz. butter
squeeze of lemon juice

Peel, core and slice apples, place in pan with water, butter and lemon juice. Simmer gently for 15–20 minutes until reduced to a pulp. Beat well with wooden spoon or press through sieve to form a purée. Serve with roast pork, grilled or fried pork sausages.

Tomato sauce

1 rasher streaky bacon
1 oz. melted butter or lard
1 small onion
8 oz. fresh tomatoes
1 bay leaf
½ pint stock (made from stock cube)
¼ level teaspoon grated nutmeg
salt
freshly ground black pepper
½ oz. cornflour
1 level teaspoon sugar

Trim rind from bacon and cut into small pieces. Fry in melted butter or lard in a pan for 2 minutes. Peel and slice onion, chop tomatoes. Add to pan with bay leaf, cover and cook gently for 5 minutes. Mix in stock, grated nutmeg, salt and ground black pepper to taste. Bring to boil, cover and simmer gently for 15–20 minutes. Pass mixture through sieve to make a purée. Return purée to pan, add cornflour which has been blended with a little extra stock or water, and the sugar. Bring to boil, cook for 3 minutes, stirring continuously. Serve with meat or fish dishes.

Mint sauce

1 handful mint leaves
1 tablespoon caster sugar
3–4 tablespoons hot water
3–4 tablespoons vinegar or lemon juice

Rinse and dry the mint leaves. Sprinkle with 1 teaspoon caster sugar and chop finely or pound in a pestle and mortar. Transfer to sauceboat, add hot water and remaining sugar. Stir until sugar dissolves, add vinegar or lemon juice. Stand for 1 hour in cold place. Serve with lamb dishes.

Horseradish sauce

1 dessertspoon vinegar
squeeze of lemon juice
½ teaspoon dry mustard
salt and pepper
¼ teaspoon sugar
1–2 heaped tablespoons freshly grated horseradish
1 small carton (2½ fluid oz.) double cream

Mix vinegar, lemon juice, dry mustard, seasoning, sugar and grated horseradish together. Whip cream till stiff. Fold in other ingredients. Add more seasoning if required. Serve with roast beef dishes, also good with some fish dishes, particularly smoked trout.

Mustard sauce

1 shallot or small onion
1 oz. melted butter or margarine
¾ oz. plain flour
scant ½ pint stock (made from chicken stock cube)
1 small bay leaf
salt and pepper
1 rounded teaspoon made mustard
a little chopped parsley

Peel and finely chop shallot or onion. Add to melted butter or margarine in saucepan and cook for 4–5 minutes. Add flour and stir over gentle heat for 2–3 minutes. Pour in stock and bay leaf. Simmer gently, stirring throughout, for 3–4 minutes. Remove bay leaf, season to taste. Stir in mustard. Add chopped parsley, or pour into sauceboat and sprinkle with parsley. Serve with herrings, egg, rabbit or white fish dishes.

Salad dressings

Mayonnaise

MAKES: $\frac{1}{2}$ PINT

1 teaspoon caster sugar
$\frac{1}{2}$ level teaspoon each salt,
   freshly ground black pepper
   and dry mustard
2 fresh egg yolks
1–1$\frac{1}{2}$ tablespoons tarragon or
   wine vinegar or lemon juice
$\frac{1}{2}$ pint pure olive, corn or
   ground-nut oil

Add caster sugar, salt, black pepper and dry mustard to egg yolks in a bowl. Mix well with a wire whisk or wooden spoon. Add tarragon or wine vinegar or lemon juice little by little from a spoon and beat well. Pour olive, corn or ground-nut oil into a measuring jug as this will indicate more easily the amount of oil which has been added. Place the bowl on a damp cloth to prevent slipping. Literally add oil drop by drop from measuring jug. (If oil is added too quickly at this stage the mayonnaise will be in danger of separating.) Beat well after each addition. After adding about one third of oil drop by drop, gradually increase flow of oil until it is being added in a thin stream, whisking or beating continuously. The consistency of the mayonnaise at this stage should be thick and glossy. If the mayonnaise is to stand a while before serving, cover with a cloth which has been wrung out in cold water to prevent a skin forming on the surface. If it is to be kept for several days before using, store in an airtight container in a very cool place or a refrigerator.

Mayonnaise Variations

Tartare

$\frac{1}{2}$ pint prepared basic mayonnaise
   (see previous recipe)
1 teaspoon each grated onion,
   finely chopped gherkins,
   capers and parsley
little finely chopped tarragon
   (optional)

Add all ingredients to mayonnaise. Serve with fish, chicken or salad dishes.

Aurore

$\frac{1}{2}$ pint prepared basic mayonnaise
   (see first recipe)
1–2 tablespoons fresh or bottled
   tomato sauce
2 tablespoons single cream
salt and pepper to taste

Add all ingredients to prepared Mayonnaise sauce. Serve as for Tartare sauce, or with egg dishes. It is also ideal for prawn cocktails.

Remoulade

$\frac{1}{2}$ pint prepared basic mayonnaise (see first recipe)
1 teaspoon each French and
   English made mustard
1 teaspoon each finely chopped
   capers, gherkins, parsley,
   tarragon (optional)
1 teaspoon anchovy essence

Add all ingredients to prepared mayonnaise. Serve with grilled meat or fish.

Wooden Spoon Club favourite

$\frac{1}{2}$ pint prepared basic mayonnaise
   (see first recipe)
1 egg white

Stiffly whisk egg white and fold in mayonnaise with a metal spoon. Use as soon as possible. Serve with potato salad or coleslaw, or with egg dishes.

French dressing

3 tablespoons olive or salad oil
1 tablespoon tarragon or wine
   vinegar
good pinch each of salt, freshly
   ground pepper, mustard and
   sugar

Place all the ingredients in a screw-top jar and then shake thoroughly. It can also be made in pestle and mortar or basin and mixed well.

French dressing Variations

Garlic dressing

1 clove of garlic
French dressing ingredients as
   previous recipe

Peel the clove of garlic, place in a mortar and crush well. Add French dressing ingredients and mix thoroughly.

Lemon dressing

French dressing ingredients, but
   using 2 tablespoons lemon
   juice, instead of vinegar
$\frac{1}{2}$ level teaspoon finely grated
   lemon rind

Make up French dressing, using lemon juice instead of vinegar, then add lemon rind.

Mint dressing

French dressing ingredients
1 tablespoon chopped mint
1 teaspoon sugar

Make up French dressing, then mix in chopped mint and sugar.

Any of these dressings may be used with Green salad, Simple salad, Gina's salad or Summer salad (see pp. 98, 99 and 101). Serve separately or add just before serving.

15 · Stuffings

Sage and onion stuffing

FOR DUCKLING, GOOSE OR PORK

1 lb. onions
2 level teaspoons dried sage
4 oz. fresh white breadcrumbs
1 level teaspoon salt
½ level teaspoon pepper
1 small beaten egg

Peel the onions and cook in boiling water for 5 minutes. Drain well and finely chop the onions. Place in a bowl with the dried sage, breadcrumbs, salt and pepper and bind with beaten egg. Use double quantity for goose.

Forcemeat stuffing

FOR TURKEY, CHICKEN OR VEAL

6 oz. fresh white breadcrumbs
3 oz. shredded suet
2 tablespoons chopped parsley
1 rounded teaspoon mixed herbs
1 teaspoon finely grated lemon rind
1 beaten egg
a little milk
salt and pepper

Place the breadcrumbs, shredded suet, chopped parsley, mixed herbs and finely grated lemon rind into a bowl. Bind together with beaten egg and a little milk if required. Season well. Sufficient for a 12-lb. turkey. Use half quantities for chicken or veal.

Mint stuffing

FOR LAMB AND MUTTON

2 oz. margarine
2 tablespoons chopped onion
8 good tablespoons fresh white breadcrumbs
2 teaspoons chopped parsley
2 tablespoons finely chopped mint
2–3 tablespoons milk
salt and pepper

Melt margarine in pan and gently fry onions. Add the breadcrumbs, chopped herbs and sufficient milk to bind. Season to taste.

Lemon stuffing

FOR PORK, VEAL OR POULTRY

1 onion
2 sticks celery
2 oz. butter
4 oz. fresh white breadcrumbs
finely grated rind of 1 lemon
2 tablespoons chopped parsley
a little beaten egg to bind
salt and pepper

Peel and chop the onion. Wash and chop the celery. Melt butter in a saucepan, add vegetables and cook gently for 5 minutes. Add breadcrumbs, finely grated lemon rind and chopped parsley, bind with a little beaten egg. Season to taste. Use double quantity for a 12-lb. turkey.

Peanut stuffing

FOR CHICKEN, TURKEY, PORK OR LAMB

1 green pepper
1 peeled chopped onion
2 oz. melted butter
6 oz. fresh white breadcrumbs
3 oz. roughly chopped unsalted peanuts
½ level teaspoon mixed herbs
1 egg
salt
freshly ground black pepper

Cut the top off the green pepper, scoop out the seeds and discard. Chop the flesh finely. Fry peeled and chopped onion and chopped pepper in melted butter for 10 minutes till tender. Remove from the heat and add the breadcrumbs, roughly chopped unsalted peanuts and mixed herbs. Bind mixture with the beaten egg. Season to taste. Sufficient for a 14–16-lb. turkey. Use half quantity for a chicken.

Apple and walnut stuffing

FOR LAMB, PORK OR POULTRY

1 onion
½ oz. hot melted butter
1 large sour cooking apple
2 oz. shelled walnuts
2 oz. pork sausagemeat or sausagemeat from 2 chipolata sausages
2 oz. fresh white breadcrumbs
½ teaspoon mixed dried herbs
salt and pepper
1 egg
milk to bind if necessary

Peel and finely chop the onion and fry in hot melted butter until pale golden brown. Peel, core and finely chop the apple. Chop walnuts. Mix all ingredients, bind with beaten egg, and milk if necessary. Use double quantity for a 12-lb. turkey.

Prune and apple stuffing

FOR LAMB, POULTRY OR PORK
6 oz. prunes
4 oz. fresh white breadcrumbs
2 large cooking apples
finely grated rind and juice of
    ½ lemon
1 beaten egg
1–2 oz. melted butter
salt and pepper

Soak prunes overnight, drain, remove stones, chop roughly. Mix with breadcrumbs, peeled, cored and chopped apples, finely grated lemon rind, and juice. Add beaten egg and melted butter to bind. Season to taste.

Celery stuffing

FOR PORK, CHICKEN OR TURKEY
6 oz. chopped celery
4 chopped onions
2 oz. melted butter or margarine
8 oz. fresh white breadcrumbs
1 tablespoon chopped parsley
1 beaten egg
2–3 tablespoons milk
salt and pepper
pinch each ground nutmeg,
    dried thyme and sage

Fry celery and onions in melted butter or margarine until soft. Put in bowl and add breadcrumbs, parsley, beaten egg, milk, seasoning and herbs. Mix until smooth. Sufficient for a 12-lb. turkey. Use half these quantities for chicken and pork.

Mushroom and bacon stuffing

FOR TURKEY
6 oz. mushrooms
6 oz. streaky bacon
6 oz. fresh white breadcrumbs
1 dessertspoon peeled chopped
    onion
½ level teaspoon mixed herbs
1 level dessertspoon chopped
    parsley
salt and pepper
2–3 oz. melted butter
3 small beaten eggs

Wash, dry and coarsely chop mushrooms. Place in a bowl. De-rind and chop the streaky bacon. Add to mushrooms together with breadcrumbs, onion, mixed herbs, chopped parsley and salt and pepper to taste. Stir in melted butter and beaten eggs. Mix well. Sufficient for a 12-lb. bird.

Herb and orange stuffing

FOR TURKEY
4 oz. fresh white breadcrumbs
2 tablespoons chopped mixed
    herbs (parsley, thyme, chives
    and marjoram)
salt and pepper
1–1½ oz. butter
2 tablespoons finely chopped
    onion
rind and juice of 1 large orange
1 small beaten egg

Mix breadcrumbs and mixed herbs with seasoning. Melt butter in saucepan, add finely chopped onion and cook for 3–4 minutes without browning. Add to crumb mixture with rind and juice of orange. Bind with beaten egg to moist consistency. Sufficient for a 7–12-lb. bird.

Sweetcorn and pimiento stuffing

FOR TURKEY OR CHICKEN
4 oz. butter or margarine
1 large peeled finely chopped
    onion
2 cans (12 oz. each) sweetcorn
    kernels
1 can (7 oz.) pimiento
finely grated rind of 2 lemons
6 oz. cornflake crumbs
2 beaten eggs
salt
freshly ground black pepper

Melt the butter or margarine in a pan and cook the peeled and finely chopped onion till tender. Drain cans of sweetcorn kernels and pimiento. Chop pimiento, mix with sweetcorn, cooked onion and melted butter, lemon rind and cornflake crumbs. Bind with eggs. Season well with salt and ground black pepper. Sufficient for a 12-lb. turkey. Use half quantity for chicken.

Chestnut stuffing

FOR TURKEY
1 lb. chestnuts
stock (made from turkey giblets)
3 oz. fresh white breadcrumbs
8 oz. pork sausagemeat
2 oz. melted butter or margarine
1 small finely chopped onion
salt and pepper

Wash chestnuts, make a split in both ends with sharp knife. Boil in water for 10 minutes and then peel, taking a few at a time from pan. Cover peeled chestnuts with giblet stock and simmer until tender. Drain well, reserving stock. Press the chestnuts through a fine sieve then add breadcrumbs, pork sausagemeat, melted butter or margarine and finely chopped onion. Season well. Mix together, adding a little of the reserved stock to moisten if the mixture is dry. Sufficient for a 12-lb. bird.

16 · Step-by-step basics

Shortcrust pastry

TO MAKE: 12 OZ. SHORTCRUST
PASTRY
12 oz. plain flour
½ level teaspoon salt
3 oz. butter or margarine
3 oz. lard or cooking fat
4 tablespoons cold water

TO MAKE: 8 OZ. SHORTCRUST
PASTRY
8 oz. plain flour
good pinch of salt
2 oz. butter or margarine
2 oz. lard or cooking fat
3 tablespoons cold water

TO MAKE: 6 OZ. SHORTCRUST
PASTRY
6 oz. plain flour
good pinch of salt
1½ oz. butter or margarine
1½ oz. lard or cooking fat
2 tablespoons cold water

STEP ONE
Keep everything as cool as possible. Sift flour and salt into bowl. Add the fats and cut into flour using a knife.

STEP TWO
Use fingertips only to rub the fats lightly into the flour to make a mixture that resembles fine breadcrumbs.

STEP THREE
Stir water in with a knife, then draw mixture together with fingers to form a firm but pliable dough. Knead gently on a lightly floured board till free from cracks.

Covering a pie dish

STEP ONE
Roll out pastry 2 inches larger than the pie dish. Hold the pie dish over the pastry as a guide. Cut off a strip about 1 inch wide, press on to dampened pie-dish rim.

STEP TWO
Brush the pastry rim with water. Fill pie dish with prepared filling. Cover with pastry lid, press edges firmly together then trim edges with knife. Knock up edges with back of knife.

STEP THREE
For a savoury pie, flute the edge by forming a series of indentations with thumb and back of knife at about 1-inch intervals. For a sweet pie flute the edge at about ¼-inch intervals.

French flan pastry

9 oz. plain flour
4 oz. slightly softened butter
4 oz. caster sugar
grated rind of 1 lemon
1 egg

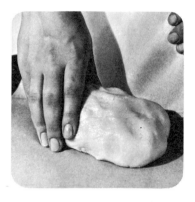

STEP ONE
Sift the flour into the centre of a board. Make a well in the centre. Add the slightly softened butter, caster sugar and grated lemon rind, then break egg into middle.

STEP TWO
Blend these ingredients together gradually drawing in the flour. Use only the fingertips of one hand. After the flour is incorporated, work to a smooth paste with the heel of the hand.

STEP THREE
Wrap the pastry in a piece of greaseproof paper and leave it in refrigerator overnight till well chilled. Allow pastry to stand at room temperature for 1 hour before using. Use to line flan see below.

Lining a flan ring

Use French flan pastry (see above) or 6 oz. Shortcrust pastry (see opposite)

STEP ONE
Stand an 8-inch fluted flan ring on a baking tray. Lightly knead the prepared pastry till smooth. Use a floured rolling pin to roll out the pastry into a 11–12-inch round on a slightly floured board. Lift the pastry carefully over the rolling pin and place over flan ring.

STEP TWO
Carefully ease the pastry into the flan ring so that it goes in neatly without creases. Press pastry into flutes. Trim off excess pastry by rolling the rolling pin over the top of the flan, remove the trimmings.

STEP THREE
Place a round of greaseproof paper or kitchen foil in the flan and weigh down with baking beans or bread crusts. Place in a moderately hot oven (375 deg. F. —Mark 5) and bake 'blind' for 15 minutes to set the pastry. Then remove the ring, paper and baking beans. Return flan to oven for a further 5–10 minutes to cook the pastry completely before filling.

Step-by-step basics

Victoria sponge
4 oz. butter or margarine
4 oz. caster sugar
2 eggs
4 oz. self-raising flour
pinch of salt
1 tablespoon warm water
jam for spreading
caster or icing sugar for top

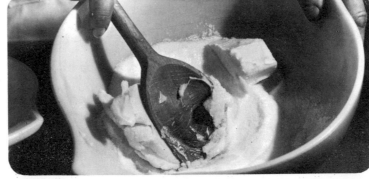
STEP ONE

STEP ONE
Grease an 8-inch sandwich tin with lard or cooking oil and dust with a little flour. Use a wooden spoon to beat butter or margarine in bowl with caster sugar until it becomes soft and fluffy.

STEP TWO
Add eggs, one at a time, beating well between each addition. Use a metal spoon to lightly fold in sifted flour with pinch of salt. Gently stir in the warm water.

STEP TWO

STEP THREE
Spread mixture evenly over prepared tin. Put just above centre of preheated moderately hot oven (375 deg. F.—Mark 5) and cook for about 20 minutes until well risen and pale golden.

STEP FOUR
Turn out sponge on wire rack and leave until cold. Use a sharp knife to cut across in half. Sandwich the two halves with jam. Sprinkle top with caster or icing sugar.

STEP THREE

STEP FOUR

Making a Swiss roll

3 oz. plain flour
1 level teaspoon baking powder
pinch of salt
3–4 tablespoons warm jam or
  lemon curd
3 eggs
4 oz. caster sugar
1 tablespoon hot water
caster sugar for dredging

STEP ONE
Grease a 9- by 12-inch Swiss roll tin and line with greased greaseproof paper. Sift flour, baking powder and salt on to a plate. Place jam in jar in saucepan of water over low heat. Place eggs and sugar in a bowl over a pan of gently steaming water. Whisk together until very thick and creamy, about 10 minutes.

STEP TWO
Remove bowl from water and continue whisking mixture until cool. Fold in flour mixture as lightly as possible with metal spoon. Lastly fold in hot water. Pour into prepared tin and tap on table to spread evenly. Bake in a hot oven (400 deg. F.— Mark 6) 7–10 minutes until pale golden and springy. Be careful not to overcook.

STEP THREE
Quickly turn out sponge on to a piece of paper well sprinkled with caster sugar. Carefully strip off lining paper. Trim off crisp edges with a sharp knife then make a shallow cut about $\frac{1}{2}$ inch from the shortest side nearest you. Spread the warm jam or lemon curd over sponge, taking it almost to edge.

STEP FOUR
Lifting the edges of the sugared paper nearest you roll the sponge into a neat, firm roll. Stand roll join side down on a cooling rack. Leave until cold, away from any draughts. Sprinkle with more caster sugar before serving. Best eaten at once, but can be stored overnight in airtight tin.

STEP ONE

STEP TWO

STEP THREE

STEP FOUR

Step-by-step basics

To almond paste and ice a Christmas cake

APRICOT GLAZE:

3–4 tablespoons apricot jam
1 dessertspoon lemon juice

ALMOND PASTE:

12 oz. ground almonds
12 oz. caster sugar
12 oz. sifted icing sugar
2 small lightly beaten eggs
1–2 tablespoons strained lemon juice
1 tablespoon sherry (optional)
½ teaspoon each vanilla and almond essences

ROYAL ICING:

3 large egg whites
1 dessertspoon strained lemon juice
approximately 1½ lb. sifted icing sugar

TO PREPARE APRICOT GLAZE:
Gently heat the apricot jam and lemon juice. Rub through a sieve into a bowl. Use while hot.

TO PREPARE ALMOND PASTE:
Mix the ground almonds, caster sugar and sifted icing sugar in a bowl. Hollow out the centre and pour in the lightly beaten eggs, strained lemon juice, sherry if using, and the essences. Mix well then knead till mixture is free from cracks, on a lightly sugared board.

TO PREPARE ROYAL ICING:
Place the egg whites and strained lemon juice in a bowl and beat to a froth with a wooden spoon. Add the icing sugar, a tablespoonful at a time, beat well after each addition. Continue . adding the icing sugar until the icing stands in firm peaks. Keep covered with a damp cloth or a piece of polythene to prevent a crust forming.

To Almond Paste Cake:

STEP ONE
Roll out half the almond paste on a lightly sugared board into a round slightly larger than the diameter of the cake. Brush top of cake with warm apricot glaze and place upside-down on prepared almond paste round. Use a palette knife to press paste into base of cake to make neat straight sides.

STEP TWO
Carefully turn cake right way up. Divide remaining almond paste in half and roll each piece into a strip the width of the cake and long enough to go halfway round; trim. Brush strips with apricot glaze, lay cake on its side at one end of strip and roll to press on paste, repeat with second and make neat joins. Place on cake board, leave 2–3 days to dry out.

To Royal Ice Cake:

STEP ONE
Place half the Royal icing on top of the cake and spread out evenly with a palette knife (meanwhile, keep remaining icing moist by covering basin with a damp tea-towel). Take a ruler and draw it gently across top of cake to make a smooth surface. Or, if preferred, smooth top with palette knife dipped in hot water.

STEP TWO
Use palette knife to spread sides of cake evenly with Royal icing. Dip knife in hot water to ease spreading. Use tip of knife to rough up surface to give snow effect round edges of cake. Wipe round edge of board. Leave 2 hours till peaks set. Fold round of greaseproof paper size of top of cake into quarters. Unfold and mark lines of fold with pencil. Place on top of cake and secure with pins.

STEP THREE
Lightly prick along pencil lines to make cross then remove paper and pipe along these lines. Make shell border round edge of cake. Allow to set before adding final festive decorations.

Making a piping bag

STEP ONE

Cut a 10-inch square of grease-proof paper diagonally in two. Hold point of triangle facing away from you and curl one end round to a point.

STEP TWO

Hold firmly in position with thumb and curl the other end round the back so that the three points of the triangle meet at top.

STEP THREE

Adjust the points, making sure that there is no open space at the end. Fold over twice to hold the bag firmly in position.

STEP FOUR

Cut off about ½ inch at end of bag and drop in required piping tube. Half fill with prepared icing and fold bag over firmly into neat fold.

TO USE

Hold the piping bag upright with the thumb of the right hand pressed lightly in the fold. The left hand supports the bag. Pressure is made with the right thumb.

Icing pattern guide

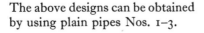

The above designs can be obtained by using plain pipes Nos. 1–3.

Borders, stars and scrolls as above can be obtained by using pipes Nos. 6, 7, 8, 13 and 15 depending on fineness of design required.

Step-by-step basics

Plain omelette

SERVES: ONE

2–3 eggs
salt and pepper
1 tablespoon water
½ oz. butter
1 tablespoon chopped parsley

STEP ONE

Break eggs into a bowl, use a fork to beat eggs lightly until well mixed, add seasoning to taste and the water. Heat the butter in a warm omelette pan until just beginning to foam, and then add all the egg mixture.

STEP TWO

Stir the mixture lightly with the back of a fork using a slow stroking motion, at the same time gently shake the pan from side to side so as to allow the uncooked egg mixture to flow underneath the cooked mixture and set.

STEP THREE

When the omelette is lightly set and the top still creamy, tilt the pan and use a palette knife to fold the omelette over. Cook a few more seconds and turn out on to a serving plate. Sprinkle with the chopped parsley.

Cheese omelette

Make up and cook the omelette as in steps one and two. Sprinkle with 1–2 oz. finely grated cheese before folding the omelette over. Continue cooking as instructed and serve.

Tomato omelette

½ oz. butter
1 small peeled chopped onion
3–4 sliced tomatoes
salt and pepper

Make up and cook the omelette as in steps one and two. Melt the butter in a pan. Cook the peeled and chopped onion till tender, about 10 minutes. Add sliced tomatoes, season to taste, heat gently for 5 minutes. Serve as an accompaniment or filling.

Mushroom omelette

4–6 oz. button mushrooms
½ oz. butter
salt and pepper

Make up and cook the omelette as in steps one and two. Wash and slice the button mushrooms. Melt butter in pan, add the mushrooms and seasoning to taste. Cover with a lid, and cook slowly till tender, about 5 minutes. Serve as an accompaniment or filling.

Coffee making

ONE PINT BLACK COFFEE SERVES: THREE TO FOUR PEOPLE
4 rounded dessertspoons pure ground coffee to each pint boiling water
hot milk and sugar to taste

STEP ONE

Heat the coffee pot. Put the rounded dessertspoons of pure ground coffee into the pot.

STEP TWO

Pour in freshly boiling water and stir. Allow to stand 1 minute.

STEP THREE

Dip a spoon into the coffee and turn over the floating grounds so that they will sink to the bottom. Allow coffee to stand for 4 minutes before straining into coffee cups. Serve with hot milk (not boiling) and sugar if desired.

198

Dressed lobster

SERVES: TWO
1 large cooked lobster
3–4 tablespoons mayonnaise
salt and pepper
TO SERVE:
lettuce
tomato wedges
watercress

STEP ONE

STEP ONE
Split lobster with sharp knife. Open halves, cut side uppermost. Remove and discard intestine (long black line running to tail). Discard lady fingers (found where small claws join body).

STEP TWO
Carefully remove stomach bag, situated near head. Reserve coral (bright pink in cooked lobster) and use to garnish or add to prepared sauce.

STEP TWO

STEP THREE
Remove the large claws, then crack with a weight. Take out the flesh from the claws in one piece if possible and add to other flesh scooped out from body of lobster.

STEP FOUR
Mix lobster meat with mayonnaise and seasoning to taste, then pile back into shells and decorate with coral. Serve on bed of lettuce, with tomato wedges and watercress.

STEP THREE

STEP FOUR

Useful facts and figures

Notes on metrication

Exact conversion from Imperial to metric measures does not give very convenient working quantities and so for greater convenience it is better to round off the metric measures into units of 25 g.
The following table shows the recommended equivalents.

Oz./fluid oz.	Approx. g. and ml. to nearest whole figure	Recommended conversion to nearest unit of 25
1	28	25
2	57	50
3	85	75
4	113	100
5 (¼ pint)	142	150
6	170	175
7	198	200
8	226	225
9	255	250
10 (½ pint)	283	275
11	311	300
12	340	350
13	368	375
14	396	400
15	428	425
16	456	450
17	484	475
18	512	500
19	541	550
20 (1 pint)	569	575

When converting quantities over 20 oz. first add the appropriate figures in the centre column, then adjust to the nearest unit of 25. As a general guide, 1 kg. (1000 g.) equals 2·2 lb. or about 2 lb. 3 oz.; 1 litre (1000 ml.) equals 1·76 pints or almost exactly 1¾ pints. This method of conversion gives good results in nearly all recipes; however, in certain recipes a more accurate conversion is necessary to produce a balanced recipe.

Liquid measures

The millilitre is a very small unit of measurement so, for ease, it is suggested that decilitres are used. In most cases it is perfectly satisfactory to round off the exact millilitre conversion to the nearest decilitre, except for ¼ pint; thus ¼ pint (142 ml.) is 1½ dl., ½ pint (283 ml.) is 3 dl., ¾ pint (428 ml.) is 4 dl. and 1 pint (569 ml.) is 6 dl. or a generous ½ litre. For quantities over 1 pint it is recommended that litres and fractions of a litre are used.

Oven temperature chart

Description	Fahrenheit	Celsius	Gas Mark
Very cool	225	110	¼
	250	120	½
Cool	275	140	1
	300	150	2
Moderate	325	160	3
	350	180	4
Moderately hot	375	190	5
	400	200	6
Hot	425	220	7
	450	230	8
Very hot	475	240	9

As different makes of cookers vary and if you are in any doubt about the setting it is recommended that you refer to the manufacturer's chart.

Notes for American users

Imperial	American
1 lb. butter	2 cups
1 lb. flour	4 cups
1 lb. granulated or castor sugar	2 cups
1 lb. icing or confectioners' sugar	$3\frac{1}{2}$ cups
1 lb. brown sugar	2 cups (firmly packed)
8 oz. stoned dates	$1\frac{1}{4}$ cups
1 lb. dried fruit	3 cups
4 oz. chopped nuts	1 cup
8 oz. glacé cherries	1 cup
4 oz. cocoa powder	1 cup
1 oz. flour	$\frac{1}{4}$ cup
1 oz. sugar	2 tablespoons
1 oz. butter	2 tablespoons

Liquid measures

$\frac{1}{4}$ pint liquid (milk, stock, water, etc.)	$\frac{2}{3}$ cup
$\frac{1}{2}$ pint liquid	$1\frac{1}{4}$ cups
1 pint liquid	$2\frac{1}{2}$ cups

The Imperial pint is 20 fluid oz. whereas the American pint is 16 fluid oz.; the British standard tablespoon holds 17·7 ml. whereas the American tablespoon holds 14·2 ml.

The following list gives American equivalents or substitutes for some terms, equipment and ingredients used in this book.

Imperial	American
Baking tin	Baking pan
Bicarbonate of soda	Baking soda
Biscuit mixture	Cookie dough
Black olives	Ripe olives
Cake mixture	Batter
Chicory	Endive
Cocoa powder	Unsweetened cocoa
Cocktail stick	Wooden toothpick
Coffee essence	Strong black coffee
Cornflour	Cornstarch
Deep cake tin	Spring form pan
Demerara sugar	Brown sugar
Desiccated coconut	Shredded coconut
Digestive biscuits	Graham crackers
Double cream	Whipping/heavy cream
Greaseproof paper	Wax or parchment paper
Glacé cherries	Candied cherries
Grill	Broil/Broiler
Ketchup	Catsup
Minced beef	Ground beef
Milk chocolate	Semi-sweet chocolate pieces
Pastry cutters	Cookie cutters
Patty tins	Muffin pans/cups
Plain flour	All-purpose flour
Self-raising flour	All-purpose flour sifted with baking powder
Single cream	Half-and-half
Sandwich cake tin	Layer pan
Sultanas	Seedless white raisins
Swiss roll (tin)	Jelly roll (pan)
Tomato purée	Tomato paste
Unsalted butter	Sweet butter
Vanilla essence	Vanilla extract

Index